ALL SHALL BE WELL

ALL SHALL BE WELL

Daily Readings from Julian of Norwich

Revelations of Divine Love

ABRIDGED AND ARRANGED

by

SHEILA UPJOHN

MOREHOUSE PUBLISHING
Harrisburg, PA

The cover illustration is the painting Lady Julian of Norwich *(1985) in the series "Revelations of Divine Love of Julian of Norwich" by the Australian artist Alan Oldfield.*

Translation and arrangement © 1992 Sheila Upjohn

First published in Great Britain by Darton, Longman and Todd Ltd

First American edition published by

Morehouse Publishing
P.O. Box 1321
Harrisburg, PA 17105

Library of Congress Cataloging-in-Publication Data:

Julian of Norwich, b. 1343.
   [Revelations of divine love. English. Selections]
   All shall be well: daily readings from Julian of Norwich/
abridged and arranged for daily reading by Sheila Upjohn.
     p. cm.
   Originally published: Great Britain: Darton, Longman, and Todd, 1992.
   ISBN 0-8192-1614-3 (pbk.)
   1. Devotional literature, English (Middle) 2. Love—Religious aspects—Christianity—Prayer-books and devotions—English.
3. Private revelations—Prayer-books and devotions—English.
4. Julian of Norwich, b. 1343. I. Upjohn, Sheila. II. Title.
BV4831.J82513   1994
242'.2—dc20
                                       93-50573
                                           CIP

Printed in the United States of America
by
BSC LITHO
Harrisburg, PA 17105

This book is for Robert Llewelyn
who made me start it
and John Michael Mountney
who made me finish it

I am most grateful to Alan Oldfield, the Australian artist who has shown me so much about Julian, for permission to use his picture of *Lady Julian of Norwich* for the cover of this book.

FOREWORD

The Revelations of Divine Love by Julian of Norwich is widely acknowledged as one of the great classics of the spiritual life. The fourteenth-century scribe who introduces Julian's book to the public graphically describes it as 'a sublime and wonderful revelation of the unutterable love of God'. The book is written, he tells us, for 'God's faithful lovers' echoing Julian's own words that she is writing 'for men and women who, for God's love, hate sin and turn themselves to do God's will'. Julian wrote throughout for the encouragement of her 'even-Christians', people like ourselves who long to know God better but who in our weakness fall frequently and need to be rescued not once but many times by his all-compassionate love. 'He is our clothing,' says Julian. 'In his love he wraps and holds us. He enfolds us in love and he will never let us go.'

No power in heaven or on earth can, in Julian's revelation and teaching, hinder God from loving us. The faithfulness and constancy of God's love, no matter how we may feel or in what state we may be, is a recurring theme in her writing. Our very falls from grace – if they can but teach us this – can be redeemed and made profitable for us. 'And through the trial of this failure', Julian would have us know, 'we shall have a high, wonderful knowledge of love in God . . . which cannot, nor will not, be broken because of wrong-doing.' And she insists on the importance of our understanding this.

Here is a book admirably catching the spirit of Julian and written with all the clarity and freshness of Sheila Upjohn's earlier translations. Its particular merit is that it offers the profound truths of Julian's writings to be savoured slowly in daily passages and thus allowed to seep into the deeper layers of the mind. By allowing ourselves to be exposed daily to the love of God, subliminal forces are called into play which, through the action of the Holy Spirit, will transform us over the years into the likeness of the one we seek. Julian's writings need to be sipped and savoured like good wine, to be meditated and pondered upon, even (perhaps especially) to be slept upon; a portion of a book such as this before sleep at night may well do more than what the doctor has prescribed.

Although the purpose of this book will be largely to nourish the spiritual life, it needs to be said that Julian is not simply a devotional writer whose book brings encouragement and hope to aspiring souls. She is, too, as is increasingly recognised today, an astute and perceptive theologian who has important things to say, and who brings new insights to the interpretation of God's love and purpose. Thomas Merton has called her a true theologian, meaning thereby that her vision of God is true, and hence that her prayer life is valid since the source is untainted by the distorted images we are prone to place upon God. Theology and devotion come together in Julian as they should always do, and the value of her book as a devotional manual springs directly out of its theological integrity. As Grace Jantzen has aptly put it, Julian 'will settle neither for an undevotional theology nor for an untheological devotion'.* Therein lies her strength as a guide to the spiritual life, and the reader may be assured that what is offered is solid food preparing the spirit through 'weal or woe' ultimately to share the vision Julian herself knew. If she can be so used she is content; she asks no more. 'You shall soon forget me,' she writes, 'and do so that I may not hinder you, and behold Jesus who is teacher of all.'

ROBERT LLEWELYN

*_Julian of Norwich: Mystic and Theologian_ (Paulist Press, 1988).

PREFACE

Julian of Norwich is a writer who has surprised everyone. Twenty years ago she was known only to a handful of people. Today her book is read all over the world, and there is a constant stream of pilgrims to her shrine, the church of St Julian in King Street, Norwich, where she lived as an anchoress and where she wrote her book *The Revelations of Divine Love*.

Julian was an unlettered woman who was granted a vision of the crucifixion on 8 May 1373. For the next twenty or so years she meditated on this, and wrote it down – perhaps having to learn to read and write in order to do so. She did this because she believed that what she had been shown was meant for all her fellow-Christians, not just for her – a belief amply borne out by the worldwide influence of her book today.

Julian's God-given understanding of the tenderness of the love of God, and of the fact that he knows no anger, is a revelation indeed after the blame and condemnation that has so often been heaped on sinners by the teaching of other generations. And her insight that, in his care for us, God looks after us as wisely as a mother looks after her children, also speaks vividly to us in the second half of the twentieth century.

I first tackled Julian's text when Robert Llewelyn asked me to translate the extracts he had chosen for *Enfolded in Love*. That little book, published like this one on 8 May, the anniversary of Julian's revelations, surprised everyone by becoming a best-seller among religious books.

Once the immediate task was over, I found myself wanting to tackle the rest of the book. So as a Lenten duty – which soon became not a penance, but a delight – I started work.

I thought then its purpose was purely private. But later it was used when Robert Llewelyn edited a second book of daily readings from Julian, *In Love Enclosed*, and again in 1989 when my own book, *In Search of Julian of Norwich*, was published, once more on 8 May.

In the meantime I had been reading and re-reading Julian's book. It struck me that the reason why so many people had been enriched by *Enfolded in Love* was that Julian needs to be taken in small measures, not downed by the pint. After all, it took her a lifetime to write, working backwards and forwards over the text, writing and re-writing, as she reached into a fuller understanding of what she had been shown. So to sit down and try to read it as if it were a novel is to be in the right place at the wrong speed – like driving through a garden on a motor bike.

I began to wonder if it would be possible to find a way to help people read the book at the right pace – to slow them down by providing frequent resting places where they could stop and reflect. Then I began to experiment to see if I could lay out the whole of Julian's book so it could be read day by day – and also so that each reading could stand on its own. But it was not until my colleague John Michael Mountney asked me if he could use my translation for his book *Sin Shall Be A Glory* that I realised the project was almost complete – and that there were now many people whose interest in Julian had been kindled by *Enfolded in Love* who might want to explore her writing further.

Editing Julian is a job where fools rush in at their peril, and I can only say that I have tried to rush as little as possible, and to be as wise as I could. I have also tried to let Julian speak as vividly in modern English as she does in medieval English, even if it sometimes means that the translation I have given is not exactly word for word. I have also had to make cuts so that each reading fits comfortably on the page. I hope that, in doing so, I have not left too many pearls on the cutting room floor.

An example of what I have done: in Chapter 17, I have omitted 'For I saw that Christ has two kinds of thirst, one bodily and one spiritual – which I shall speak of in Chapter 31. The words "I thirst" were shown me because of his bodily thirst, and I understood the cause of it was lack of moisture. For the blessed flesh and bones were dried right out and left without any blood and moisture.' Reluctant as I was to lose it, Julian does deal with this fully later on.

I have also made extensive cuts in Chapter 51, the allegory of the Lord and the servant, reducing it by about one third, and losing such sentences as: 'A double meaning was shown in the lord, and a double meaning was shown in the servant. One part was shown spiritually with actual people, the other part was shown more spiritually still, with no people present.'

Julian is writing with her usual meticulous accuracy, and in making cuts I have had to make a judgement between the rival merits of depth and brevity. Always I have been conscious that any omission is a loss.

But if such a loss helps make Julian's book more accessible, and so brings the message of God's love to more of her twentieth-century fellow-Christians, then I rejoice – and hope with all my heart that Julian herself is rejoicing with me.

SHEILA UPJOHN

ALL SHALL BE WELL

These revelations were shown to an unlettered woman in the year of our Lord 1373, on the 8th day of May. This woman had asked for three gifts from God. The first was to understand his Passion; the second was to have an illness in her youth, when she was thirty years old; the third was to have, by God's grace, three wounds.

As to the first, I thought I already knew something of Christ's Passion, but I wanted to know even more, by God's grace. I wished I had been there with Mary Magdalene, and those others who were Christ's friends. And so I asked for an actual sight – through which I should have more understanding of the compassion of our Lady and all his friends who saw his agony and pain at that time.

The second petition came to my mind as I repented of sin. I asked for an illness so close to death that I might, in that illness, receive the last rites of the church; that I myself should believe I was dying – and so should everyone round me. For I wanted to loose my hold on earthly life.

These two petitions, for the Passion and the illness, I asked with a condition, saying this: 'Lord, you know what I desire, but I desire it only if it is your will that I should have it. If it is not your will, good Lord, do not be displeased, for my will is to do your will.'

As for the third petition, by God's grace and the teaching of holy church, I was filled with an overwhelming desire to receive the wound of true repentance, the wound of suffering as Christ suffered, and the wound of seeking God with all my strength. I made this petition without any conditions.

The other two desires passed from my mind, and the third was with me continually.

CHAPTER 2

[1]

And when I was thirty and a half years old, God sent me an illness which held me three days and three nights. On the fourth night I received the rites of holy church and did not think to live until day. And after this, I lingered on two days and two nights. And on the third night I often thought I was dying, and so did those who were with me. And, young as I was, I thought it was sad to die – not because of anything on earth I wanted to live for, and not because of any pain I was afraid of – for I trusted God's mercy – but because if I had lived I should have been able to love God better and for longer, so that I should know God better and love him more in the joy of heaven.

And so I thought: 'Good Lord, if I live no longer, may it be to your glory!'

And so I lasted until day, and by then my body was dead from the waist down, as I felt. Then I asked to be propped upright, leaning on others, so I should have more freedom in my heart to be at God's command and to think on God for as long as my life should last.

My priest was sent for to be at my end, and by the time he came, my eyes were set and I could not speak. He held the cross before me and said: 'I have brought you the likeness of your Maker and Saviour. Look upon it, and draw comfort from it.'

After this, my sight began to fail, and it was all dark around me in the room as if it were night, except for the cross. I saw it glow with light and I did not know how.

Then suddenly it came to my mind that I should ask that my body might be used to give me knowledge and understanding of his blessed Passion.

CHAPTER 3

At this, suddenly I saw the red blood trickle down from under the crown of thorns – hot and fresh and flooding out, as it did at the time of his Passion when the crown of thorns was pressed into his blessed head – he who was both God and man and who suffered for me. And I knew in my heart that he showed me this without any go-between.

And in this same Showing suddenly the Trinity filled my heart full of joy.

And I was astounded at the wonder of it, that he, who is so high and holy, will be so homely with a sinful soul living in frail flesh.

This sight of the blessed Passion, with the knowledge of God I felt in my mind, I knew was strength enough for me – yes, and for all living creatures – to conquer all the fiends of hell and spiritual temptation.

In this, he brought our blessed Lady to my mind. In my mind's eye I saw her as if she breathed – a simple, humble girl, not much more than a child – the age she was when she conceived.

God showed me, too, in part, the wisdom and truth of her soul, so that I understood the reverence she felt before God her Maker, and how she marvelled that he would be born of her – a simple soul that he Himself had made.

It was this wisdom and truth in her that showed her the greatness of her Maker and the smallness of herself whom he had made. And it was this that made her say so humbly to Gabriel: 'Behold God's handmaid.'

By this I know surely that she is higher in worth and grace than anyone that God has made. For, as I see it, no one is above her, except the blessed manhood of Christ.

CHAPTER 4

[3]

At this time our Lord showed me an inward sight of his homely loving. I saw that he is everything that is good and comforting to us. He is our clothing. In his love he wraps and holds us. He enfolds us in love and he will never let us go.

And then he showed me a little thing, the size of a hazelnut, in the palm of my hand – and it was as round as a ball. I looked at it with my mind's eye and I thought: 'What can this be?' And answer came: 'It is all that is made.' I marvelled that it could last, for I thought it might have crumbled to nothing, it was so small. And the answer came into my mind: 'It lasts, and ever shall, because God loves it.' And so all things have being through the love of God.

In this little thing I saw three truths. The first is that God made it. The second is that God loves it. And the third is that God looks after it.

We need to know how small creation is, and to count all things that are made as nothing, if we are to love and have God who is not created. For this is the reason we are not at rest in heart and soul – that here we seek rest in things that are so little there is no rest in them – and we do not know our God who is all-mighty, all-wise, and all-good. For he is true rest.

God's will is that we know him, and it rejoices him when we rest in him. For all that is less than him cannot satisfy us.

'God, of your goodness, give me yourself, for you are enough for me. There is nothing less I can ask that is worthy of you, and if I ask for anything less I shall be always lacking, for only in you I have all.'

For his goodness encompasses all his creatures, and all his blessed works. He has made us for himself alone, and has restored us by his blessed Passion, and keeps us in his blessed love. And he does all this through his goodness.

CHAPTER 5

[4]

Then the way we often pray came into my mind and how, through lack of knowing and understanding of the ways of love, we make use of intercessors. Then I saw truly that it gives more praise to God, and more delight, if we pray directly to him in his goodness and cling to it by his grace (with true understanding and steadfast belief) than if we made use of all the intercessors that heart can think of.

For if we create all these go-betweens it is too little and not full worship to God, for his goodness is whole and entire, and it lacks nothing.

For the goodness of God is the highest prayer that reaches right down to our lowest needs. It awakes our soul and brings it to life, and makes it grow in grace and virtue. It is closest to our nature and the surest way to grace, for it is the selfsame grace that our soul searches for – and must always search for – until we truly know the God who enfolds us.

A man walks upright, and the food of his body is sealed as in a well-made purse. When the time of his necessity comes, it is opened and sealed again most properly. And that it is God who does this is shown where he says that he comes down to the lowest part of our need.

For he does not despise what he has made, nor does he disdain to serve our humblest earthly needs. For he loves the soul he has made in his likeness.

CHAPTER 6

For as the body is clad in the clothes, and the flesh in the skin, and the bones in the flesh, and the heart in the breast, so are we clothed, body and soul, in the goodness of God and enfolded in it. Yes, and more fully, for all these wither and waste away.

But the goodness of God is always whole, and closer to us beyond comparison. Our lover wants our soul to cling to him with all its might, and that we should ever hold fast to his goodness. For this above all pleases God and strengthens the soul.

For the love that God most high has for our soul is so great that it outstrips our understanding. No one on earth can comprehend how much, how sweetly and how tenderly our Maker loves us.

And so, by his help and grace, we may evermore stand in spiritual contemplation – and may wonder at this high, overflowing, immeasurable love that almighty God has for us through his goodness.

For our inborn will is to have God, and the goodwill of God is to have us. So there is no end to our willing and longing until we know God in the fullness of joy. Then our desire is filled. He wills that our occupation shall be in striving to know and love him until we are made whole in heaven.

This is why this lesson of love was shown and all the rest, as you shall see. For the strength and groundwork of all the other Showings was shown in the first. This above all causes the soul to seem small in its own sight – to see and love its Maker. And this is what fills it with reverent fear and true humility, and with generous love towards our fellow-Christians.

CHAPTER 6

[6]

Our Lord showed me our Lady, St Mary to teach us this: that it was the wisdom and truth in her, when she beheld her Maker, that enabled her to know him as so great, so holy and so mighty and so good.

His greatness and his nobleness filled her with reverent fear. She saw herself so little and so low, so simple and poor compared with God that she was filled with humility. And so from this humbleness she was lifted up to grace and all manner of virtues, and stands above all.

While he showed what I have just set down to my inward sight, in my outward sight I saw Christ's head bleeding fast. The great drops of blood fell down from under the crown of thorns like pellets, as though they burst out of the veins. As it came out, it was brownish red, for the blood was very thick. As it spread, it became bright red, and when it reached the brows it vanished. Even so, the bleeding lasted long enough for me to see and understand many things.

It was so lovely and lifelike that there is nothing to compare it with. It was as plentiful as the drops of water that fall from the eaves after a great shower of rain, that fall so thick and fast no one can count them. And for roundness, they were like the scales of herring as they spread on the forehead.

This Showing was vivid and lifelike, hideous and dreadful, sweet and lovely. And in all this sight it was enormous comfort to me that our God and Lord, who is so holy and mighty, is also so homely and courteous. And this filled me full of happiness and certainty of soul.

CHAPTER 7

He gave me a plain example of how to understand this: a mighty king or a great lord gives the greatest honour to a humble servant if he is companionable with him, and if he himself, both privately and publicly, shows that he really means it and delights in it.

Then the poor servant thinks: 'How could this great lord do me more honour and give me more pleasure than to show me, who am so humble, this wonderful friendship? Truly it gives me more pleasure and happiness than if he gave me rich gifts and was aloof and cold.'

And so it is with our Lord Jesus and us. For truly it is the highest joy that can be, as I see it, that he who is highest and mightiest, noblest and worthiest, is yet lowest and gentlest, most homely and most courteous.

And in deed and in truth, this overflowing joy shall be given to us all when we see him. And this is our Lord's will – that we trust and believe, joy and delight, comfort and cheer ourselves (as we can with his grace and help) until the time comes when we see this for certain.

But this great companionship no man may know in this life on earth, unless he has it by special Showing from God, or by a great outpouring of grace given inwardly by the Holy Ghost.

But faith and belief, with love, deserve this reward, and it may also be got by grace. For our life is grounded in faith, together with hope and love.

And when this Showing, which is given in time, is finished and folded away, then the Faith keeps it fresh, by the grace of the Holy Ghost, until our life's end. And it is nothing but the Faith – no more and no less – that brings this about.

CHAPTER 7

I understood six things from this Showing:

The first is the sign of the blessed Passion and the plentiful shedding of his precious blood.

The second is the maid who is his most dear mother.

The third is the blessed godhead that ever was, and is and ever shall be – all power, all wisdom and all love.

The fourth is everything that he has made – for I knew well that heaven and earth and all that is made is big and huge, but the reason it seemed so little in my sight was because I saw it in the presence of him who is the Maker of all things. For if a soul sees the Maker, all that is made seems small indeed.

The fifth is that he made all things for love – and that they are cherished by that same love and shall be, without end.

The sixth is that God is everything that is good, as I see it, and the goodness that is in everything is God.

In all this I was greatly stirred in love for all my fellow-Christians, for I wanted them to know and see the same that I saw, so it would comfort them. For this sight was shown for all the world.

Therefore I pray you all, for God's sake, and I tell you for your own good, that you do not let your eyes dwell on the humble woman this was shown to, but let your sight go beyond – and wisely, humbly and mightily behold God who, by his courteous love and endless goodness, wishes it to be widely known to comfort us all.

CHAPTER 8

Because of this Showing, I am not good. I am only good if I love God better. If you love God better than I do because of it, it does you more good than me. I do not say this to those who are wise, for they know it well, but I say it to you who are simple to cheer and comfort you – for we all need comfort.

For truly it was not shown to me that God loved me better than he loves the humblest soul that is in grace – for I am sure there are many who never had either Sign or Showing, except for the ordinary teaching of holy church, who love God better than I do.

For if I look at myself alone, I am nothing. But when I think of myself and my fellow-Christians joined together by love, I have hope. For in this joining lies the life of all who shall be saved.

For God is all that is good, as I see it, and God has made all that is made, and God loves all that he has made. And he who loves all his fellow-Christians, for God's sake, loves all that is. (And he who loves thus, loves all.)

For in mankind who shall be saved everything is included – that is to say, all that is made and the Maker of all. For in man is God, and God is in all. And I hope, by the grace of God, he who understands this shall be truly taught and comforted, if he has need of comfort.

CHAPTER 9

I speak of those who shall be saved, for at this time God showed me no others. But in everything I believe as holy church believes, preaches and teaches. For the faith of the church (which I had already understood and, as I hope, had by the grace of God willingly followed and accepted) was constantly in my mind. I never meant, nor wanted, to receive anything that was contrary to it. And with this in my mind I looked upon the Showing with all my strength. For in this blessed Showing I saw God's meaning was all one with the Faith.

All this was shown in three ways: that is to say, by outward sight, and by words formed in my mind, and by inward sight. But the inward sight I neither can, nor may, show as plainly nor as fully as I should like. But I trust in our Lord God almighty that he shall, in his goodness, and for love of you, help you to understand it more inwardly and more joyfully than I can or am allowed to tell it to you.

CHAPTER 9

And after this, in my outward sight, I saw a part of his Passion in Christ's face on the cross – which was in front of me, and on which I looked continually. I saw how he was scorned, and spat on, and sullied and beaten – and many long-drawn agonies (more than I can tell you) and how the colour of his face often changed.

And once I saw how half his face, beginning at the ear, was covered over with dried blood until it reached the centre. And after this, the other half became covered with blood in the same way as the first half cleared. I saw this with my outward sight, dimly and darkly, and I asked for better light, so as to see more clearly.

And I was answered in my mind: 'If God wills to show you more, he will be your light. You have need of none but him.' For I saw him while I sought him.

For here we are so blind and foolish that we never look for God until he, in his goodness, shows himself to us. When we see something of him, through his grace, then we are guided by the same grace to seek him with great longing, and to see him more joyfully.

And so I saw him and I sought him. I had him and I lacked him. And this is, and should be, our usual way, as I see it.

CHAPTER 10

At one time my mind was led down to the bottom of the sea. And there I saw hills and green valleys looking as if they were covered with moss and with seaweed and sand. Then I understood this: that if a man or a woman were under the wide waters, as long as he could still see God (and God is with us always) he should be safe in body and soul and take no harm. And over and above this, he would have more cheer and comfort than all the world can tell.

For he wills that we believe we can see him all the time continually, even though it seems to us we see him very little. When we believe this, he helps us all the time to get grace. For his will is to be seen and to be sought – his will is to be waited for and trusted.

This second Showing was so humble, so small and simple, that my spirit was in great distress as I looked at it – sorrowful, fearful and worried. For part of the time I doubted whether it was a Showing at all.

And then, many times, our good Lord gave me an insight to know that it truly was a Showing.

CHAPTER 10

It was a token and likeness of our dark cloak of sin that our beautiful, bright, blessed Lord wore for our sake. It made me think of the holy handkerchief in Rome which he has imprinted with his own blessed face when he was in great suffering, embracing death at his own will – and which often changes colour.

Many people marvel at the brownness and blackness, the sadness and thinness of the likeness – when they know that he who marked it with his blessed face is the glory of heaven, flower of earth and fruit of the Virgin's womb. Then how should this image be so discoloured and so far from fair?

I want to tell what I have understood by the grace of God. We know in our Faith, and believe by the preaching and teaching of holy church, that the blessed Trinity made mankind in his image and in his likeness.

In the same way we know that when man fell so deep and so sadly into sin there was no other way to restore him except through Him that made man. And He who made man, for love, by that same love would restore man to his first bliss – and more besides.

And as we were made like the Trinity when we were first made, so our Maker wills that, when we are re-made, we should be like Jesus Christ our Saviour, in heaven without end. Then, between these two, he would – for love and honour to men – make himself as like to man in this mortal life, in our dirt and wretchedness, as man can be without sin.

CHAPTER 10

So the meaning of this is what has already been said: it was the token and likeness of our dark cloak of foul black deeds that hid our beautiful, bright, blessed Lord.

But I dare to say full surely, and we should believe it, that there never was so fair a man as he, until his brightness was clouded by toil and sorrow, suffering and dying. And this Showing was to teach me that when the soul continually seeks God, it pleases him greatly.

For the soul can do no more than seek, suffer and trust – and this is the work of the Holy Spirit in the soul. And the clearness in finding him comes by his special grace, when it is his will. This seeking with faith, hope and love pleases our Lord, and the finding pleases the soul and fills it full of joy.

And so I was taught in my mind that seeking is as good as seeing during the time he lets the soul labour.

And he himself shall teach a soul how it may come to have a sight of him. And this is most glory to him and profit to you, and the richest way to receive meekness and virtue by the guidance of the Holy Ghost.

For a soul that entirely clings to him with true trust – either of seeking or seeing – is the highest worship it may bring him, as I see it.

CHAPTER 10

There are two works that can be seen in this Showing: one is seeking, the other is seeing.

The seeking is common to all – that is, every soul can have by his grace – and ought to have – the discernment and teaching of holy church.

It is God's will that we have three things in our seeking.

The first is that we seek willingly and actively, without sloth (as we can through his grace), gladly and happily, without foolish sadness and empty sorrow.

The second is that we wait upon him steadfastly for love, not grumbling and striving against him, until our life's end – for it lasts so short a time.

The third is that we trust him completely with certainty of faith. For it is his will that we know he will come suddenly and joyfully to all who love him. For his way is secret, his will is to be seen, his coming shall be right sudden, and his will is to be trusted. For he is gracious and homely. Blessed may he be!

CHAPTER 10

And after this I saw God in a point, that is, in my mind's eye. And I thought: 'What is sin?' For I saw in truth that God does all things, no matter how small they may be. And I saw that nothing happens by chance, but by the far-sighted wisdom of God. If it seems like chance or accident to us, it is because we are blind and blinkered.

For the things planned by God since before the world began (which he rightly and gloriously and continually shapes to the best end as they come about) come upon us suddenly and take us unawares. And so in our blindness and short-sightedness we say these are accident or chance. But to our Lord God they are not so.

Therefore I needs must grant that everything that is done, is done well, for it is God that does all.

For he is the still point at the centre. There is no doer but he. And I was sure he did no sin. And here I saw truly that sin has no substance, for in all this there was never a sight of sin. And so the rightfulness of God's work was shown to my soul.

Rightfulness has two good properties: it is right and it is complete – and so are the works of our Lord God. They need the operation of neither mercy nor grace, for they are complete and lack nothing.

This Showing was made to my understanding because our Lord wills the soul should be truly turned to look upon him and on all his works in general. For they are wholly good, and all that he does is comforting and sweet, and brings great ease to the soul that is turned from the blind judgement of man to the kind judgement of our Lord God.

CHAPTER 11

[17]

For a man sees some deeds as good and some deeds as evil, but our Lord God does not see them so. For all that has being in nature is of God's making, so everything that is done has the nature of God's doing.

For it is easy to understand that the best deed is well done. But the smallest deed is done just as well as is the best and highest. And all is done in the manner and in the order that our Lord has ordained for it since before the world began.

For there is no doer but He.

I saw surely that he never changes his purpose for anything, nor ever shall, without end, for ever.

For from the beginning nothing was unknown to him in his rightful intent. And so everything was set in order, before anything was made, as it should be for ever – and nothing shall fall short of its purpose.

For he made all things in the fullness of goodness. And therefore the blessed Trinity is always fully pleased with all his works.

All this he showed me in great joy, saying: 'See, I am God. See, I am in all things. See, I do all things. See, I never take my hands off my work, nor ever shall, through all eternity. See, I lead all things to the end I have prepared for them. I do this by the same wisdom, and love, and power through which I made them. How can anything be done that is not done well?'

Thus was the soul deeply, wisely and lovingly searched by this vision. Then I saw truly that it is right that I should assent to it with great reverence, rejoicing in God.

CHAPTER 11

And after this, as I looked, I saw the body bleeding freely from the weals made by the scourging. The fair skin was driven deep into the tender flesh by the harsh striking all over the sweet body.

The warm blood ran out so freely that there was neither skin nor wounds to be seen but, as it were, all blood. And the bleeding, as I saw it, was so plentiful that I thought that if it had been real and substantial it would have soaked the bed with blood and flowed all around it.

And then it came into my mind that God has made many waters in earth for our use and our comfort, because of his dear love for us. But yet it pleases him better that we should simply and humbly take his blessed blood to wash away our sins.

For there is no liquid he likes so much to give us. The most dear blood of our Lord Jesus Christ is as precious as it is plentiful – look and see.

The precious plenty of his dear blood went down into hell and broke its bonds and delivered all those who were there who belonged to the court of heaven.

The precious plenty of his dear blood overflows all the earth and waits to wash away the sin of all people who are of good will.

The precious plenty of his dear blood went up to heaven to the blessed body of our Lord Jesus Christ and is there with him, bleeding and praying for us to the Father – and is and shall be for as long as it is needed.

CHAPTER 12

And after this, before God spoke any word, he allowed me to look upon him for a while. And all that I had seen and all the meaning of it was there, as far as the simplicity of my soul could understand it. Then he, without words or opening his lips, formed these words in my soul: 'By this is the fiend overcome.'

In this our Lord showed that it is his Passion that is the fiend's undoing. God showed that the fiend has the same malice now as he had before the incarnation. And, hard as he works, so he continually sees that all the souls of salvation escape him, gloriously, by virtue of Christ's Passion. And this is his sorrow, and he is put down, full of evil.

For all that God allows him to do turns to joy to us, and shame and woe to him. And he has as much pain when God gives him leave to work as when he is idle. And this is because he can never do as much evil as he would like, for his power is all taken into God's hands.

But in God there is no anger, as I see it. For our good Lord always has in his mind his own goodness and the rewarding of those who shall be saved. He sets his might and his right in the path of the Evil One who, for wickedness and malice, busies himself to plot and work against God's will. Also, I saw our Lord scorn the devil's malice and expose his lack of power – and he wills that we should do so, too.

CHAPTER 13

Because of this sight I laughed aloud and made those who were round me laugh too, and their laughing rejoiced my heart. I wanted all my fellow-Christians to see what I saw, so they would all laugh with me.

But I did not see Christ laugh, although I understood that we may laugh aloud in comforting ourselves, and rejoicing in God because the devil is overcome.

And after this I became serious and said: 'I see three things – joy, scorn and truth. I see joy that the fiend is overcome. I see scorn because God scorns him and he shall be scorned hereafter. I see truth in that he is overcome by the blessed Passion and death of our Lord Jesus Christ, which was done in truth and with hard labour.'

I thought of Judgement Day and of all those who shall be saved, whose happiness he greatly envies. For at that day he shall see that all the grief and trouble he has brought upon them shall be turned into even greater joy for them, without end. And all the pain and tribulation he wished upon them shall go with him to hell, without end also.

CHAPTER 13

And after this our good Lord said: 'I thank you for your labour, and especially for your youth.' And my mind was lifted up to heaven where I saw our Lord as a lord who has asked all his much-loved servants and friends to a great feast. Then I saw the lord did not sit in state in one place, but ranged royally through the whole house, filling it full of joy and laughter. He himself, courteously and companionably, greeted and delighted his dear friends with love shining from his fair face like a marvellous melody that has no end.

God showed three kinds of joy that every soul that has served God willingly on earth shall have in heaven.

The first is the wonderful thanks of our Lord God, which shall be his as soon as he is delivered from this world's pain. This thanks is so great and glorious that he will think it fills him to the brim, even if there were no more to come. For I thought that all the toil and trouble that all mortal men together could suffer would not be enough to deserve the glorious thanks that just one man shall have who has served God willingly.

The second kind of joy is that this glorious giving of thanks shall be seen by all the blessed souls that are in heaven. For God makes a man's service to him known to all the heavenly host. And then an example of this was shown me: if a king thanks his servants, it is great praise to them. But if he makes it known throughout his kingdom, then the glory is that much greater.

The third kind of joy is this: That the freshness and delight of that moment shall last for ever.

CHAPTER 14

And I saw this simply and sweetly shown: That every man's age shall be known in heaven, and he shall be rewarded for his willing service and for the length of time he has given it. And particularly those who freely and willingly offer their youth to God shall be specially rewarded and wonderfully thanked.

For I saw that no matter when, or for how long, a man or woman is truly turned to God, even for one day's service given with his whole will, he shall have all three kinds of joy without end.

And the more a loving soul sees this graciousness of God, the more he wants to serve him all the days of his life.

CHAPTER 14

And after this he put a most high inward happiness in my soul. I was filled full of endless certainty, and it was sustained so strongly that it left no room for doubts and fears. This feeling was so happy and so holy, and put me in such peace and rest, that there was nothing on earth that had the power to make me sad.

This lasted only a while and then my mood was changed, and I was left on my own in sadness and weariness of life. I loathed myself so much that I could hardly bear to live.

There was nothing to comfort me or give me any ease except for faith, hope and love. And although I knew them to be true, they gave me little joy.

And soon after this our blessed Lord gave me again that comfort and rest of soul, so blissful and so mighty in its sureness and delight that no fear, no sorrow, and no bodily pain that I might suffer could have taken away my peace.

And then the sadness once more overcame my mind, and then the joy and gladness – now the one, now the other – I suppose about twenty times.

And in the time of joy I might have said with St Paul: 'Nothing shall separate me from the love of Christ.' And in the sadness I might have said with St Peter: 'Lord save me, for I perish.'

CHAPTER 15

This vision was shown me, as I understand it, because it is necessary for some souls to feel in this way – sometimes to know comfort, and sometimes to fail and be left on their own. God wants us to know that he keeps us safe through good and ill.

For his soul's sake a man is sometimes left on his own, but his sin is not always the cause. For during this time I did not sin, so why should I have been forsaken – and so suddenly? Also I did nothing to deserve this feeling of bliss.

But our Lord freely gives what it is his will to give, and sometimes lets us suffer woe – and both are part of one love. For bliss is lasting and pain is passing, and shall come to nothing for those who shall be saved.

And therefore it is not God's will that we should linger over pain with sorrow and sadness, but that we should pass quickly through it to joy without end.

CHAPTER 15

And after this, Christ showed me the part of his Passion when he was near to death. I saw his dear face drained of blood, dry, as it were, and pale as death. Then it grew paler still with death and suffering. Then as death came closer it turned blue, and then a bluish brown as life ebbed from the flesh.

For that day when our Lord and blessed Saviour died upon the cross, there was a dry, frosty wind, as I saw it. And when all the precious blood that could, had bled out of his dear body, yet there was still moisture in his dear flesh, as I was shown. Loss of blood and pain dried it from within, and wind and cold dried it from without, and both met together in Christ's body. And these four, two within and two without, dried Christ's flesh in the process of time.

And although the pain of it was sharp and bitter, it was also long drawn out, as I saw it, and agonisingly dried out all the living essence of Christ's flesh. So I saw his dear flesh die, part by part, as it seemed, drying out with dreadful pain.

The pain was so long drawn out that it seemed to me as if he had been seven nights dead, dying, at the point of death, enduring those last pains. When I say it was as if he had been dead a week, I mean that his dear body was so discoloured, so dried out, so withered, so deathlike and so pitiful that he might have been seven nights dead, and dying every one. And I thought the dying of his flesh was the last and most painful part of his Passion.

CHAPTER 16

As I saw this dying, the words of Christ came into my mind: 'I thirst.'

The blessed body hung alone there and dried for a long time, and the nails wrenched it as the weight of the body pulled against them. For I understood that, because of the softness of the tender hands and feet, the huge, hard, hurtful nails pulled the wounds wide open. And the body sagged with the weight of its long hanging.

And there was piercing and wrenching of the head, and the binding of the crown of thorns – all caked with dried blood with the sweet hair twined in it – dried flesh sticking to the thorns and thorns to the dying flesh.

And at first, while the flesh was new-cut and bleeding, the constant pressure of the thorns made the wounds gape wide. And I saw, too, the sweet skin and tender flesh, with its hair and blood, was all raised and loose above the bone because of the thorns.

The thorns had stabbed it into pieces, so that it sagged like a cloth. I did not see how the wounds were made, but I understood it was by the sharp thorns and by the way the crown was crammed on, roughly and harshly – hard and without pity.

The flesh began to dry and lose some of its weight and began to set round the crown of thorns – and so it circled it about, like one crown upon another.

The crown of thorns was stained with blood and the other crown and the head were the same colour – the colour of dried blood. The skin of the flesh that sagged from the face and body was full of small wrinkles and was a tanned colour, like a dry scorched board, and the face was browner than the body.

CHAPTER 17

I saw four kinds of drying. The first was loss of blood. The second was the pain that followed. The third was through hanging in the air, as women hang out clothes to dry. The fourth was that his mortal flesh craved moisture and no one administered comfort to him in all his woe and agony. Ah! hard and grievous was his pain, but much more hard and grievous it grew when the moisture ebbed and all began to dry out and wither.

These were the pains that showed in his blessed head. As for the pains I saw, all that I can say is too little, for it cannot be talked of.

This Showing of Christ's pain filled me full of pain, for though I knew well he suffered only once, yet it was his will to show it me and fill my mind with it, as I had often asked before.

Then I thought: 'I little knew what pain it was I asked for,' and like a fool regretted it, thinking that if I had known what it would be like, I should not have prayed to suffer it. For I thought this pain was worse than death itself, my pain.

I thought: 'Is any pain like this?' and I was answered in my mind: 'Hell is a different pain, for there, there is despair. But of all the pains that lead to salvation, this is the greatest – to see the one you love suffer.'

How could any pain be worse to me than to see him suffer who is my whole life, my whole bliss and my whole joy? Then I knew truly that I loved Christ so much more than myself that there could be no pain like the grief I had to see him suffer.

CHAPTER 17

Here I saw part of the compassion of our Lady, St Mary, for she and Christ were so joined in love that the greatness of his love caused the greatness of her grief. And so, in this, I saw the instinctive love, led on by grace, that all creation has for him.

Here I saw a great communion between Christ and ourselves, as I see it, for when he was in pain, we were in pain. And all creation capable of feeling pain suffered with him.

The firmament, the very earth itself, began to lose their nature with sorrow at the time of Christ's dying. For it is part of their nature to know and acknowledge him from whom their virtue springs as their God.

So when his strength left him, their strength left them too, in sympathy, as far as it could, in grief at his pain. And so those who were his friends suffered pain because they loved him. And all men in general — that is to say, even those who did not know him — had to bear the loss of every kind of comfort, except for the deep, quiet keeping of God.

God in his goodness makes the nature of the planets and elements in tune with the nature of both the blessed man and the cursed. But in that time this harmony was withdrawn from both kinds of men — and so it came about that even those who did not know him were in sorrow then.

And so was our Lord Jesus made nothing for us, and we are all made nothing with him — and shall be nothing until we come to his bliss, as I shall tell hereafter.

CHAPTER 18

And then I wanted to look away from the cross, and I dared not. For I knew well that while I looked at the cross I was safe and sure. I did not want to put my soul in peril, for there was no safety from the terrors of devils, except for the cross.

Then I heard a word in my ear that said to me, like a friend: 'Look up to heaven to his Father.'

Then I saw clearly by faith that there was nothing between the cross and heaven that could have done me any harm. Either I had to look up or to answer.

I answered inwardly with all my soul's strength and said: 'No, I cannot, for you are my heaven.' This I said because I did not want to look away – for I had rather have borne that pain until the Day of Judgement than come to heaven by any other way than through him. For I knew well that he who bound me so fast could unbind me when he chose.

So I was taught to choose Jesus for my heaven, though I saw him only in pain at that time. I wanted no other heaven than Jesus, who shall be my joy when I come there. And this has always been a comfort to me, that I chose Jesus as my heaven, by his grace, in this time of Passion and sorrow. And it has been a lesson to me that I should always do this – choose only Jesus as my heaven, in joy and in sorrow.

CHAPTER 19

And though, like a fool, I wanted to turn back – I said before that if I had known what the pain would be like I should not have prayed to have it – here I saw truly that this was the grumbling and groaning of the flesh, not of the soul, which God gives us no blame for.

I wanted to turn back and I wanted to press forward, both at the same time. These opposites are two separate things – one outward and one inward.

The outward part is our mortal flesh which is now in pain and woe and always shall be in this life. I felt this outward pain greatly at this time and that part wanted to turn back. The inward part is the high, happy life which is all peace and love – and this I felt inwardly. And it was in this part that greatly, wisely and willingly I chose Jesus for my heaven.

And by this I saw truly that the inward part is master and king of the outward part. It does not need the will or bidding of the outward part, but all the inward will and intent is settled for ever to be joined with our Lord Jesus. Whether the outward part can draw the inward to agree with it was not shown me, only that the inward draws the outward by grace, and both shall be joined in joy without end through the virtue of Christ – this was shown.

CHAPTER 19

And so I saw our Lord Jesus lingering on a long time – for the joining of godhead and manhood gave the manhood strength to suffer more for love than all men together could have borne. I do not mean only more pain than all men could suffer, but also that he endured more pain than all those who shall be saved – from the first beginning to the last day – could tell, count, or imagine – bearing in mind the worth of the highest glorious king and the shameful, despised and painful death.

For he that is highest and most glorious was counted less than nothing and utterly despised. For the deepest truth of the Passion is to know and understand who he was that suffered.

For as much as he was pure and loving, even so much was he strong and able to suffer – for it was the sin of every man that shall be saved that he suffered for. And he saw the sorrow and desolation of every one of us, and grieved over it for love because he shared our nature. For as greatly as our Lady grieved over his pain, he grieved for her grief just as much – and more, because the manhood he bore was of even greater worth.

And I, seeing all this through his grace, saw that the love he has for our soul is so strong that he sought our soul with great longing, and willingly suffered for it – and paid for it in full.

For a soul that looks on these things shall see, when it is touched by grace, that the pains of Christ's Passion go beyond all other pain and, true to tell, that these same pains shall be turned into endless joys through Christ's Passion.

CHAPTER 20

It is God's will, as I see it, that we should look upon his blessed Passion in three ways.

The first is the great pain he suffered, and we should look on it with sorrow for our sins and compassion with him. And this is the way our Lord showed me at that time, and gave me strength and grace to see it.

And I looked for the moment of his death with all my strength and thought to have seen his body quite lifeless, but I did not see him so. And just at the same moment, it seemed, that I thought that life could last no longer and the sight of his end must be shown, suddenly, as I looked on that same cross, his expression changed to joy.

This change in his blessed mood changed mine, and I was as glad and merry as can be. Then our Lord brought this gladly into my mind: 'Where is any part of your pain and grief now?' And I was overjoyed.

I understood that our Lord means that in this life we are on his cross with him in our pain and sorrow and our dying, and that if, of our own free will, we stay on that cross, with his help and grace, until the last moment, suddenly his expression will change and we shall be with him in heaven.

Between the one and the other there shall be no lapse of time, but at once everything shall be changed to joy.

CHAPTER 21

And this is what he meant when he said to me: 'Where is any part of your pain and grief now?' And we shall be wholly blessed. And here I saw truly that, if he showed us his blessed expression now, there is no pain on earth, nor in any other place, that could grieve us. But everything would fill us with joy and gladness.

But since he shows us the time of his Passion and his cross which he bore in this life, this is the reason why we are sad and troubled with him – as our frail flesh needs must be.

And the reason why he suffers is that it is his will, in his goodness, to make us heirs with him of his joy. And, in exchange for this little pain that we suffer here, we shall have a high, endless knowledge in God, which we could never have had without it.

And the harder has been our pain with him on the cross, the higher will be our honour with him in his kingdom.

CHAPTER 21

Then our good Lord Jesus Christ said: 'Are you well paid by the way I suffered for you?' I said: 'Yes, Lord, I thank you. Yes, good Lord, blessed be your name.'

Then said Jesus, our kind Lord: 'If you are well paid, I am well paid, too. It is a joy, a happiness, an endless delight that ever I suffered my Passion for your sake. If I could have suffered more, I would have suffered more.'

In understanding this, my mind was lifted up to heaven, and I saw three heavens, and greatly wondered at the sight. And I thought: 'I see three heavens and all are encompassed in the blessed manhood of Christ – none is more, none is less, none is higher, none is lower – but all equally alike in blessedness.'

The first heaven Christ showed me was his Father, not in bodily form, but in his nature and his way of working. That is to say, I saw in Christ what the Father is. The way that our Father works is this – that he awards honour to the Son, Jesus Christ. This gift and this reward is so full of joy to Jesus that his Father could not have given him any recompense that could have pleased him better.

For the Father is fully pleased with all the deeds that Jesus has done to win our salvation. Through this we are his, not just because he bought us, but also by the gracious gift of his Father we are his joy, his reward, his glory and his crown by the generous gift of his Father.

CHAPTER 22

This was a great marvel and a most sweet sight – that we are his crown. This that I tell is such great joy to Jesus that his sorrow and his grievous Passion and his cruel, shameful death seem nothing to him. And through these words: 'If I could have suffered more, I would have suffered more,' I saw truly that, however many times he could have died, he would have died. And love would never let him rest until he had done it.

And I looked with great diligence to know how many times he would die if he could, and truly the number was so far beyond my understanding that my mind had not the space or strength to comprehend it. And when he had died as many times as this, yet he would still think it nothing for love. For everything seems small to him when it is set beside his reward of love.

For though the dear manhood of Christ could suffer only once, the goodness that is in him can never cease from offering itself again. Every day he is ready to suffer again, if it could be.

For if he said he would make a new heaven and a new earth for love of me, this would deserve little reward. For he could do this every day if he wished, without any toil or trouble. But to die for love of me so many times that the number is too huge to reckon – this is the highest offer that our Lord God can make for man's soul, as I see it.

CHAPTER 22

So he means this: 'How can it then be that I would not do all that I could for your love? The deed does not grieve me, since I would willingly die as often as this and think nothing of my hard pain.'

And here I saw, for the second time in this Showing of the Passion, that the love that made him willing to suffer is as far above the pains that he bore as the heaven is above the earth. For bearing the pain was a noble, honourable deed that was accomplished by the working of love at a certain time.

But the love had no beginning, it is now, and it shall have no ending. And because of this love he said these words so tenderly: 'If I could suffer more, I would suffer more.' He did not say 'If there was any need to suffer more', for though there was no need, if he could suffer more, he would.

These deeds and these words to win our salvation were ordained as perfectly as God could order them.

And here I saw that Christ's joy is complete, for his joy could not have been complete if there was any other way the work could have been done better.

CHAPTER 22

And in these words: 'It is a joy and happiness and an endless delight to me', three heavens were shown me. The joy was, I understand, the pleasure of the Father. The happiness was the honour of the Son. And the endless delight was the Holy Ghost. The Father is pleased, the Son is honoured, and the Holy Spirit is full of delight.

And here I saw a third truth in his blessed Passion – that is, the joy and happiness that makes him delight in it.

For it is God's will that we should rejoice with him in our salvation and that we should be cheered and strengthened by it. He wants our soul to delight in its salvation, through his grace. For we are his joy. He delights in us for ever as we shall in him, by his grace.

And all that he has done for us, and is doing, and shall do, was never a charge or burden to him, nor could it be. He paid a price only for the deeds he did while he wore our flesh – that is to say, beginning from his precious incarnation and lasting until his joyful rising from the dead on Easter Day.

Jesus wills we understand the joy the blessed Trinity has in our salvation, and that we open our hearts and rejoice just as much – so that our joy should be as much like Christ's own joy as it can be while we are still here on earth.

CHAPTER 23

The whole Trinity was at work in the Passion of Christ, bringing overflowing virtue and grace to us through him. But it was the Virgin's son alone who suffered. And so the whole Trinity is filled with joy through this.

And in this he brought the nature of a cheerful giver to my mind. A cheerful giver does not count the cost of what he gives. His heart is set on pleasing him to whom the gift is given. And if he who receives it takes the gift with joyful thanks, then the courteous giver thinks it has cost him nothing compared with the joy and happiness he has had in pleasing and delighting the one he loves. Fully and truly was this shown.

Ponder also on the weight of this word 'ever'. It shows the height of love Christ knew in our salvation, and the manifold joys that follow from his Passion.

One is, that he rejoices that he has accomplished it in fact and that he shall suffer no more. Another is that he has brought us up to heaven and made us his crown and endless joy. Another is that by it he has bought us from the endless pains of hell.

CHAPTER 23

Then with a happy face our Lord looked into his side, and saw what was there, and rejoiced. And with this look he helped my understanding to look through the wound to what lay within.

And then he showed a fair and lovely place, large enough for all mankind that shall be saved to rest in peace and love. And in this he brought to my mind the dear blood and precious water which he let pour out for love. And in this dear sight he showed his blessed heart split clean in two.

And also, so that I should understand better, these words were spoken: 'Look how I loved you. Look and see that I loved you so much before I died for you that I was ready to die for you, and now I have died for you, and suffered of my own free will so I could do it. And now all my bitter pain and agony is turned into endless joy for you and me. How could it be that now you should ask me anything that pleases me and I should not grant it you? For my pleasure is your holiness and in the endless joy and bliss you share with me.'

This, as simply as I can tell you, is the meaning in these blessed words: 'Look how I loved you.' Our good Lord showed us this to make us glad and happy.

CHAPTER 24

And with this same look of joy and happiness, our Lord looked down to his right, and made me remember where our Lady stood at the time of his Passion. And he said: 'Would you like to see her?'

And in these sweet words it was as if he said: 'I know full well that you would like to see my blessed mother, for she is the greatest delight, after myself, that I could show you – the one dearest to me and the one who gives me highest praise. She is most worth seeing of all that I have made.'

And, so that we should understand even better, our Lord speaks to all mankind who shall be saved as if they were just one person – as though he said: 'Can you see in her how you yourself are loved? It was for love of you that I made her so high, so noble and so good. And this brings me great joy – and I want it to bring you joy, too.'

But in all this I was not taught to wish to see her bodily presence while I am here on earth, but to want to understand the virtues of her soul – her truth, her wisdom and her love. Through understanding this I can learn to know myself and reverently praise God.

CHAPTER 25

[41]

And when our Lord had shown me this and had said in these words: 'Would you like to see her?', I answered and said: 'Yes, good Lord, if it is your will.'

I prayed this many times, and I thought to have seen her in bodily presence, but I did not see her so. And in his words, Jesus showed me an inward sight of her, and just as, before, I had seen her little and simple, so now he showed her high and noble and glorious – and more pleasing to him than all else in creation.

And he wills it to be known that all those who delight in him should also delight in her – and in the delight he has in her, and she in him. And he showed this example to help us understand: that if a man loves one being above all the rest, then he will make all the rest love and delight in the one he loves so much.

And in those words that Jesus said: 'Would you like to see her?', I thought it was the most loving thing he could have said to me about her.

For our Lord showed me nothing else in particular except our Lady, St Mary, and he showed her to me three times. The first time was when she was with child, the second was as she was in her sorrow under the cross, the third, as she now is in delight, worship and joy.

CHAPTER 25

And after this our Lord showed himself more glorious, in my sight, than I ever saw him before – by which I was taught that our soul shall never have rest till it come to him, knowing that he is the fullness of joy – homely and courteous, blessed and life itself.

Our Lord Jesus said again and again: 'It is I, it is I. It is I that am highest. It is I that you love. It is I that you enjoy. It is I that you serve. It is I that you long for. It is I that you desire. It is I that you mean. It is I that am all. It is I that holy church preaches and teaches. It is I that showed myself here to you.'

The number of the words goes beyond my wit and understanding and all my might, and it is the highest, as I see it. For in this is gathered in – I cannot tell, but the joy that I saw in the Showing of it goes beyond all that the heart may want or the soul may desire. And therefore these words are not set down here, but every man, with the grace that God gives him in understanding and loving, will receive our Lord's meaning himself.

CHAPTER 26

And after this, the Lord brought into my mind the longing that I had for him before. And I saw that nothing stood in my way but sin. And I saw this was the same for all of us.

And it seemed to me that, if sin had not been, we should all have been clean and like unto our Lord, the way he made us. And so, in my folly, before this time, I had often wondered why, by the great foreseeing wisdom of God, the beginning of sin was not prevented – for then, I thought, all should have been well.

I should have left off this worrying, but nevertheless I mourned and sorrowed over it without reason or discretion. But Jesus, who in this Showing told me all that I needed, answered by this word and said: 'Sin is behovely – it had to be – but all shall be well, and all shall be well, and all manner of thing shall be well.'

In this stark word 'sin' our Lord brought to my mind all things in general that are not good – and the shame, the despising and the utter stripping he accepted for us in this life – and his dying. He also brought to mind all the bodily and spiritual pains and passions of all his creatures.

For we are all stripped in part – and shall be – while we follow our master Jesus, until we are made pure. That is to say, until we are stripped of our mortal flesh and of all our inner desires that are not really good.

CHAPTER 27

And all this was shown in a moment and was quickly turned to comfort, for our Lord God does not want the soul to be frightened by this ugly sight. But I did not see sin. For I believe it has no kind of substance or manner of being, and that it is only known through the pain it causes. And as for pain, it is something, as I see it, that is only for the time being, for it cleanses us and makes us know ourselves and ask forgiveness. And throughout all this the Passion of our Lord comforts us, and it is his blessed will it should do so.

And because of our good Lord's tender love to all those who shall be saved, he quickly comforts them, saying: 'The cause of all this pain is sin. But all shall be well, and all shall be well, and all manner of thing shall be well.'

These words were said so kindly, and without a hint of blame to me or to any who shall be saved. So how unjust would it be for me to blame God for allowing me to sin, when he does not blame me for falling into it.

And in these words I saw a wonderful high secret hidden in God – and that he will show us this secret openly in heaven. When we know this secret, we shall truly see the reason he allowed sin to be, and in the knowledge of this we shall rejoice endlessly in our Lord God.

CHAPTER 27

So I saw that Christ has compassion on us because of sin. And just as, before this, I was filled with pain and compassion during Christ's Passion, in the same way I was filled full of compassion for all my fellow-Christians – those much, much-loved people who shall be saved, that is to say. For God's servants, holy church, shall be shaken in sorrow and anguish and tribulation in this world, as a cloth is shaken in the wind. And, as to this, our Lord answered in this way: 'I shall make a great occasion out of this in heaven, of endless honour and everlasting joy.'

Yes, I saw so much that I understood that our Lord, in his pity and compassion, can be pleased by his servants' tribulation. He lays upon every one he longs to bring to his bliss something that is no blame in his sight, but for which they are blamed and despised in this world – scorned, mocked and cast out. He does this to offset the harm they should otherwise have from the pomp and vainglory of this earthly life, and to make their road to him easier, and to bring them higher in his joy without end.

For he says: 'I will shatter all your vain affections and your vicious pride, and after that I shall gather you up and make you kind and gentle, clean and holy, by joining you to me.'

CHAPTER 28

And then I saw that every feeling of kinship and compassion that a man feels, in love, for his fellow-Christians, it is Christ within him.

His willingness to be accounted nothing, which was shown in his Passion, was shown over again in his compassion. And there are two ways to understand our Lord's meaning in this.

One is the bliss we are brought to, which he wants us to rejoice in. The second is to comfort us in our pain – for it is his will that we should know that our pain shall be all turned to honour and gain by virtue of his Passion – and that we should understand that we do not suffer alone, but with him.

He wills that we see him as the ground we grow in, and that we see his pains, and his being counted worthless, go so far beyond anything we can suffer that it cannot be imagined.

Knowing this will save us from grumbling and from despair as we suffer our pain. And even if we truly see that we deserve it, yet his love excuses us, and in his great courtesy he does away with all our blame. And he upholds us in compassion and pity, as if we were children, innocent and eager.

CHAPTER 28

But I stayed pondering, in grief and sorrow. In my mind I said this to my Lord, in fear and trembling: 'Oh, good Lord, how can all be well when great harm has come to your creatures through sin?' And here I wanted, if I dared, to have some clearer explanation to put my mind at rest.

And to this our blessed Lord answered very gently, with a most kind look, and showed that Adam's sin was the worst harm that was done, and ever shall be, until the world's end. And he also showed that this is clearly known by all holy church on earth.

More than this, he taught me I should look on the glorious Atonement. For this making amends was more pleasing to God, and more helpful for the salvation of many, without compare, than ever the sin of Adam was harmful.

What our Lord means by this teaching is that we should remember this: 'Since I have brought good out of the worst evil, I want you to know, by this, that I shall bring good out of all lesser evils, too.'

CHAPTER 29

He gave me understanding of two separate things. One is our Saviour and our salvation. This blessed part is open and plain, and lovely and clear and abundant – for all mankind that is of goodwill, now and henceforth, is included in this part.

Our Lord wants us to occupy ourselves with this part, rejoicing in him because he rejoices in us. And the more wholeheartedly we do this, with humble reverence, the more thanks we have, and the more we gain from it. And so we can see and rejoice that the Lord is our portion.

The second part is hidden and shut away from us, for it is beside our salvation. It is our Lord's private concern, and it is proper to the royal kingship of God that he should be able to keep his own counsel in peace. And it is proper to his servant, out of obedience and reverence, that he should not pry into his affairs.

Our Lord has pity and compassion on us because there are some busybodies who meddle with such things. But I am sure that if we knew how much we should please him and ease ourselves if we left them alone, we would do so.

The saints that are in heaven want to know nothing except what our Lord wants to show them, and their love and their desire is also ruled by our Lord's will. And so we ought to make our wills like their wills. Then we shall want nor desire nothing except what is our Lord's will, as they do. For we and they are one in God's sight.

CHAPTER 30

And so our good Lord answered all the doubts and questions I could raise, saying so comfortingly: 'I am able to make all things well. I know how to make all things well, and I want to make all things well, and I shall make all things well. And you shall see for yourself that all manner of things shall be well.'

When he says 'I am able to' I understand this to be the Father. And when he says 'I know how to' I understand this to be the Son. And when he says 'I want to' I understand this to be the Holy Spirit. And when he says 'I shall' I understand the whole of the blessed Trinity – three persons and one truth. And when he says 'you shall see for yourself' I understand the gathering up together of all mankind who shall be saved into the blessed Trinity.

And in these five sayings the circle of God will be complete in rest and peace, and by this the spiritual thirst of Christ shall be ended.

For this is the spiritual thirst of Christ – a love-longing to have us all gathered together and made whole in him to his great joy, as I see it. For we are not now as wholly joined to him as we shall be then.

CHAPTER 31

We know by our faith, and also it was shown in all this, that Jesus Christ is both God and man.

Concerning the godhead. He himself is the highest bliss, and was before time began, and shall be without end. And this endless bliss can never, by its nature, be either higher or lower.

Concerning Christ's manhood. We know by our faith, and it was also shown, that he by the strength of godhead, suffered pains and Passion, for love, to bring us to his joy, and died.

And this is the joy of Christ's works, and this is what he means when he says that we are his joy, we are his reward, we are his glory, we are his crown.

Concerning Christ as our head, he is glorified and above suffering. But he is not yet glorified and above suffering in his body – in which all his members are knit. For he shall always suffer the same thirst he had on the cross – the thirst, longing and desire which was in him since before time began, as I see it. That thirst he has still, and shall have, until the last soul that is to be saved has come up into his bliss.

For as surely as there is a property of pity and compassion in God, just as surely there is in God the property of thirst and longing. And because of the strength of Christ's longing we must long for him in return – and no soul gets to heaven without it.

And so he has pity and compassion on us, and he has a great longing to have us. But his wisdom and his love will not let the end come until the time is ripe.

CHAPTER 31

At one time our good Lord said: 'All things shall be well.' And another time he said: 'You shall see for yourself that all manner of thing shall be well.' The soul understood several things from these two sayings.

One was this – that it is his will that we should understand that not only does he take care of great and noble things, but also of little and humble things, simple and small – both one and the other. And this is what he means when he says 'all manner of thing shall be well'. For he wants us to understand that the smallest thing shall not be forgotten.

Something else I understood was this – that we see such evil deeds done, and such great harm caused by them, that it seems to us that it is impossible that any good should come out of them. And we look on them, sorrowing and mourning over them, so that we cannot find rest in the joyful sight of God, as we ought to.

The trouble is this – that the range of our thinking is now so blinkered, so little and small, that we cannot see the high, wonderful wisdom and power and goodness of the blessed Trinity. And this is what he means when he says 'you shall see for yourself that all manner of thing shall be well'. It was as if he said: 'Have faith, and have trust, and at the last day you shall see it all transformed into great joy.'

CHAPTER 32

And so in these last five words set down earlier, 'I am able to make all things well, etc.', I understand a great comfort in all the works of our Lord God that are to come.

There is a Great Deed which the blessed Trinity shall do at the last day, as I see it. And what that Deed shall be, and how it shall be done, is unknown to all creatures below Christ. And it shall be hidden until it is done.

But he wants us to know of it, so that we shall be more at ease in our soul, and at peace in our love, and that we should leave off looking at all the storms that might keep us from the truth, and should rejoice in him.

This is the Great Deed, ordained by our Lord since before time began, treasured and hidden in his blessed breast, known only to him, by which he shall make all things well.

For just as the blessed Trinity made all things out of nothing, so the same blessed Trinity shall make good all that is not well.

CHAPTER 32

I marvelled greatly at this sight, and looked at our Faith, wondering thus. Our Faith is grounded in God's word, and a root of our Faith is that we believe that God shall keep his word in all things. And one point of our Faith is that many creatures shall be damned, as the angels who fell from heaven through pride are now devils. And men on earth who die out of the faith of holy church – that is to say, those who are heathens, and also those who have received the Christian faith but lived unchristian lives, and so die without love – all these shall be damned to hell without end, as holy church teaches me to believe.

And, understanding all this, I thought it was impossible that all manner of thing should be well, as our Lord showed me at this time. And I had no other answer from our Lord God in these Showings except this: 'What is impossible for you is not impossible for me. I shall keep my word in all things, and I shall make all things well.'

So I was taught by the grace of God that I should hold steadfastly to the Faith, as I had already understood it, and also that I should soberly believe that all things shall be well, as our Lord showed me at that time.

For this is the Great Deed that our Lord shall do, and in this Deed he shall keep his word in all things – that he shall make good all that is not well.

And how it shall be done, there is no creature beneath Christ who knows, nor who shall know, until it is done. This is the understanding of our Lord's meaning I had at this time.

CHAPTER 32

And in all this I asked, if I dared, to be given a clear sight of hell and purgatory. By this I did not mean to try to prove any article of faith, for I believed steadfastly that hell and purgatory exist for the same reason that holy church teaches. But I wanted to see so that I could be taught in everything that concerns the Faith, so that I might live with more glory to God and profit to me.

But although I asked to see this, I saw nothing at all – except as is set down earlier, where I saw that the devil is reproved of God and damned without end.

I took this to mean all people who are in the devil's condition in this life, and who die in that state. There is no more mention made of them in the sight of God and his holy ones than there is of the devil – notwithstanding they are of mankind and whether they have been christened or not.

CHAPTER 33

For I saw the Passion of Christ in several Showings – and while I was able to share, in part, the feelings and sorrows of our Lady and his true friends, I never saw the Jews who did him to death pointed out. Nevertheless I knew, through my Faith, that they were cursed and damned for ever, except those who were converted through grace.

And I was strengthened and taught generally to hold fast to the Faith at every point, and to everything I had been taught up to this time.

And it is God's will that we should pay great regard to all the deeds he has done already, but that we should leave off looking for what the Deed to come shall be. We should want to be like our brethren who are saints in heaven, who want nothing except what is God's will.

Then we shall delight only in God and shall be richly rewarded both in what is shown and what is hidden.

For I saw our Lord's meaning clearly – the more we busy ourselves to know his secrets in this or any other thing, the further we shall be from finding out.

CHAPTER 33

Our Lord showed two kinds of secrets. One is this Great Secret, with all the hidden things that go with it. And his will is that we should understand that they are hidden until the time comes when he will show them to us clearly.

The other kind of secrets are those he wants to make open and plain to us, for it is his will that we know them. They are secrets to us, not because he wills they shall be secrets, but because of our blindness and ignorance.

And he has great pity and compassion on us because of this. And so he will show them to us himself even more plainly, so that we may know him, and love him, and cling to him. For with kindly courtesy our Lord will show us everything that is a help for us to know, and he shows it through this – the preaching and teaching of holy church.

For he is holy church. He is the ground, he is the substance, he is the teaching, he is the teacher, he is the taught, he is the end. He is the reward for which every true soul works – and this is known and shall be known to every soul to whom the Holy Ghost declares it.

All this that I have said, and more that I shall say, is a strength against sin. For in the third Showing, when I saw that God does all that is done, I saw no sin – then I saw that all is well. But when God showed me about sin, then he said: 'All shall be well.'

CHAPTER 34

And when God had shown me his goodness so fully and freely, I asked to know whether someone I loved would go on living the holy life which I hoped he had, by the grace of God, begun. And it seemed to me that, by wanting to know this one thing in particular, I hindered myself. For I was taught nothing in this time.

And then I was answered in my mind, as if by a kindly go-between: 'Look for the courtesy of God – and see it – in things in general, as he has already shown you. For it gives more praise to God to see him in all things than in one special thing.'

I accepted this, and by this I learned that it is more praise to God to understand all things in general, than to set your heart on one thing in particular.

And if I am to live wisely by this teaching, not only should I not set too much store by any one thing, but I should also not be too distressed by any one thing, either – 'for all shall be well'.

The fullness of joy is to see God in all things. For our Lord continually draws all things to the end which he has ordained for them – by the same might, wisdom and love by which he made them. And he himself shall bring it about, and when it is time, we shall see it.

CHAPTER 35

All that our Lord does is rightful, and all that he allows is praiseworthy. And in these two, both good and evil are included.

Everything that is good is done by our Lord, and everything that is evil is done under his sufferance. I do not say that evil is praiseworthy, but that our Lord's allowing it is praiseworthy. In this his goodness shall be known for ever, by his loving-kindness and by the power of his mercy and grace.

Rightfulness is when a thing is so good that it cannot be bettered. For God is rightfulness itself, and all his works are done rightfully – just as they have been ordained since before time was – by his great might, his great wisdom, his great goodness.

And, just as he has ordained the best, so he works continually and brings it to perfection. He is always fully pleased with himself and all his works, and the sight of his blessed contentment is very sweet to the soul that sees it by grace.

All souls that shall be saved in heaven without end are made rightful in God's sight – and by his goodness. And we, above all creatures, are kept in this rightfulness – wonderfully and for ever.

CHAPTER 35

Mercy is a work that springs from the goodness of God, and it will continue to work until sin is no longer allowed to trouble faithful souls.

And when sin no longer has licence to pursue, then the work of mercy will cease. Then shall every soul be gathered into goodness, and rest there for ever.

Under his watchfulness we fall. By his blessed love and strength and wisdom we are defended. And through mercy and grace we are lifted up to many joys.

And he wills that we know and love him for his rightfulness and for his mercy – now and for ever. And the soul who sees this, through grace, shall be well pleased, and delight endlessly in both.

CHAPTER 35

Our Lord showed that a deed shall be done, and that he himself shall do it, and even though I do nothing but sin, my sin shall not stop his goodness working.

This deed shall be begun on earth, and it shall be full of praise for God and full of profit for those on earth who love him. And, as we come to heaven, we shall see it with great joy – and it shall go on being done until the last day. And the praise and joy of that deed shall continue in heaven before God and all his holy ones for ever.

This deed was shown joyfully – meaning that I should accept it wisely, faithfully and trustingly. But what the deed should be was kept secret from me.

And in this I saw that it is not his will that we fear to know the things he shows us, for he wants us to know them. It is his will that, by knowing them, we should love him, and delight in him, and rejoice in him for ever.

And because of the great love he has for us, he shows us all that is praiseworthy and profitable for us at this time. And as for the things he wills should at present be secrets to us, in his great goodness he shows us that they are hidden.

And he wills that we should believe and understand this Showing until the time we see it truly in his endless bliss.

CHAPTER 36

This is the meaning of this teaching. That this deed shall be done for me – that is to say, for everyone – for all who shall be saved. This deed shall be full of praise and wonder and shall be unstinted – and God himself shall do it. And it shall be the fullest joy there is, to see the deed that God himself shall do, while man does nothing but sin.

And this is what our Lord means. It is as if he said: 'Look and see. Here you have cause for humbleness. Here you have cause for love. Here you have cause to know yourself. Here you have cause to rejoice in me. So rejoice in me, for my love, because you can do nothing that pleases me better.'

For as long as we live here on earth, whenever we, in our folly, turn to look on the damned, our Lord touches us tenderly and calls us kindly, saying in our soul: 'Forget this fancy, much-loved child. Turn to me. I am enough for you. Rejoice in your Saviour and your salvation.'

But this deed, and that other Deed that I spoke of, are not both one, but two separate things. But this deed shall be done sooner, at the time we come to heaven – and we may know something of it here on earth, if God grants it.

But the Great Deed, spoken of before, shall be known neither in heaven nor on earth until it is done.

CHAPTER 36

Moreover, he gave this special teaching on how to understand the purpose of miracles, as if he said:

'It is known that I have done miracles on earth before this time, many and plenty, high and wonderful, praiseworthy and great. And I do the same thing now as I have done before, and shall do the same again in the time to come.'

It is well known that sorrow and anguish and troubles go before miracles. And that is why we should acknowledge our weakness and the wickedness we have fallen into through sin, so that we should humble ourselves before God, and fear him, and cry for help and grace.

Miracles follow on from this, by the great strength and wisdom and goodness of God. They show his strength, and as much of the joy of heaven as we can know in this passing life – and so they serve to strengthen our faith and increase our hope – through love.

And this is why it pleases him to be known and worshipped through miracles.

CHAPTER 36

God brought into my mind that I should sin, and because of the joy I had in looking on him, I was reluctant to look on this Showing. But our Lord was patient with me, and gave me grace to listen.

And this Showing I took as shown to me personally, but by all the healing comfort that followed, as you shall see, I was taught to see it was meant for all my fellow-Christians, and in general, and not for any one person in particular.

And I was filled with quiet fear, but our Lord answered: 'I will hold you securely.' These words were said with more love, more certainty and spiritual comfort than I am either able or allowed to tell you.

For as clearly as I was shown that I should sin, just as clearly was the comfort shown – the safekeeping of all my fellow-Christians. For what can make me love my fellow-Christians more than to see that God loves all who shall be saved as if they were all one soul?

For in every soul that shall be saved there is a godly will that never agreed to sin, and never shall. Just as there is a beastly will in our lower nature that cannot will any good – so there is a godly will in our higher nature. And this will is so good that it can never will any evil, but only good. And this is why he loves us, and why what we do always pleases him.

By this our Lord showed the wholehearted love he has for us – yes, that he loves us as much now while we are here on earth as he shall when we stand before his blessed face. And all our troubles come because our own love fails us.

CHAPTER 37

[64]

Also God showed that sin shall not be a shame to man, but a glory. For just as every sin brings its own suffering, by truth, so every soul that sins earns a blessing by love. And just as many sins are punished with much suffering, because they are so bad, even so shall they be rewarded by many joys in heaven because of the suffering and sorrow they have caused here on earth.

For the soul that comes to heaven is so precious to God, and the place so holy, that God in his goodness never allows a soul that shall finally reach there to sin, unless the sin is to be rewarded – and made known for ever, and blessedly restored by overwhelming worship.

In this Showing my understanding was lifted up to heaven. And then God brought happily into my mind David, and others without number from the Old Covenant. And in the New Covenant he brought to my mind first Mary Magdalene, Peter and Paul, Thomas of India and St John of Beverley – and also others without number. And he showed how the church on earth knows of them and of their sins – and it is no shame to them, but is all turned to their glory.

And so our courteous Lord showed them as an example of how it is in part here on earth, and shall be fully in heaven. For there, the mark of sin is turned to honour.

CHAPTER 38

As for St John of Beverley, our Lord showed him high in honour to comfort us by his homeliness, and brought to my mind how he is a near neighbour, and well known to us.

And God called him 'St John of Beverley' as plainly as we do, with a glad and happy look, showing that he is a most high saint in his sight – and a blessed one.

And in this he mentioned that, in his youth and early years, St John of Beverley was a loyal servant of God, humbly loving and fearing him – and that, nevertheless, God allowed him to fall. But he mercifully upheld him, so that he did not perish nor lose any time.

And afterwards God lifted him up to much more grace. Because of the repentance and humility he had in his life, God has given him many joys in heaven, which go beyond those he would have had if he had not fallen. On earth God shows that this is so by the many miracles that happen continually near his body.

And all this was shown to make us glad and happy in love.

CHAPTER 38

Sin is the sharpest lash that any soul can be struck with. It is a lash that thrashes men and women and makes them loathsome in their own sight, so that for a while they think themselves worthy of nothing but to sink down into hell.

But then repentance comes to them by the touch of the Holy Spirit, and turns their bitterness to hope for God's mercy. Then he begins to heal their wounds, and the soul begins to wake from death as it turns towards the life of holy church.

The Holy Spirit leads the sinner to confession, and to acknowledge his sins willingly, openly and truthfully – with great sorrow and with great shame because he has defiled the fair face of God.

Then he undertakes a penance for every sin as laid down by his confessor, who is grounded in holy church by the teaching of the Holy Spirit.

This is one form of self-abasement which pleases God greatly. Others are bodily illness sent by God, also sorrow and shame that are put upon us, and reproof, and the world's contempt – together with all kinds of troubles and temptations we fall into, both bodily and spiritual.

CHAPTER 39

Our Lord holds us tenderly when it seems to us that we are nearly forsaken and cast away because of our sin – and that we deserve to be.

And, because we are made humble by this, we are raised high in God's sight, by his grace – and also by repentance, and compassion, and true yearning for God. Then sinners are suddenly delivered from sin and from pain, and are taken up to heaven – and even made high saints.

Repentance makes us clean. Compassion makes us ready. And yearning for God makes us worthy.

Though the soul is healed, God still sees the wounds – and sees them not as scars but honours. And so, by contrast, as we have been punished here with sorrow and penance, we shall be rewarded in heaven with the courteous love of our Lord God almighty. It is his will that no one who comes there shall lose a whit of his labour.

For he looks on sin as sorrow and anguish to those who love him and, because he loves them, does not blame them for it.

CHAPTER 39

The reward we receive shall not be small – but it shall be high, glorious and full of praise. And so shame shall be turned to honour and increase of joy.

For our courteous Lord does not want his servants to fall into despair even when we fall into sin. For our falling does not stop him loving us.

Peace and love are always alive in us, but we are not always alive to peace and love. But he wills that we understand this – that he is the ground of our whole life in love, that he is our everlasting protector, who mightily defends us against our enemies who fight so hard and fiercely against us.

And we need his help all the more because we give them an advantage by our failures.

CHAPTER 39

This is a princely friendship of our courteous Lord, that he tenderly protects us, even while we are in sin. He touches us secretly, and shows us our sin by the kindly light of mercy and grace.

When we see ourselves so foul, we believe that God is angry with us because of our sin. Then, through repentance, the Holy Spirit leads us to prayers and to longing with all our hearts to mend our lives, so that God's wrath will be quenched. We do this until we find rest for our soul and ease in our conscience. Then we hope that God has forgiven our sins – and indeed he has.

Then our courteous Lord shows himself to the soul with gladness and delight, with welcoming friendship, as if the soul has been released from pain and prison, saying tenderly: 'My darling, I am glad you have come to me. In all your sorrow I have been with you always, and now you know my love and we are joined in joy.'

And this is how sins are forgiven by mercy and grace, and our soul is received in joy – just as it will be when it comes to heaven, whenever this comes about by the gracious working of the Holy Spirit, and by virtue of Christ's Passion.

Here I understood truly that whenever we are in peace and love, we are saved in fact.

CHAPTER 40

But then, because of all this spiritual comfort that has been shown, a man or woman might be led, through folly, to say or think: 'If this is true, then it is good to sin so as to get a better reward', or else to think sin less sinful. Beware of this thinking. For truly if this thought comes, it is untrue and comes from the enemy of that true love that shows us all this comfort.

This same blessed love teaches us that we should hate sin simply for the sake of love. And I am sure, by what I feel myself, that the more every soul that is true to its nature sees of this, in the courteous love of our Lord, the less it wants to sin, and the more it is ashamed.

For if all the pains of hell, and of purgatory, and of earth were laid before us – death and the rest – and were set against sin, we ought to choose to bear all those pains rather than sin. For sin is so vile, and so greatly to be hated, that it can be likened to no other pain – unless that pain is sin.

And I was shown no harder hell than sin. For there is no hell except sin for a soul that is true to its nature.

CHAPTER 40

If we turn our will to love and humbleness, the work of mercy and grace makes us bright and clean. God has as much goodwill towards man, to save him, as he has strength and wisdom. For Christ himself is the ground of all the laws of Christian men, and he taught us to do good to overcome evil.

By this we can see that he himself is love, and that he shows us what to do by doing it himself. For it is his will that we should be like him in wholeness of endless love towards ourselves and our fellow-Christians.

And just as he does not stop loving us because of our sin, so he wills that we should not stop loving ourselves or our fellow-Christians – but that we should nakedly hate sin, and love the soul for ever as God loves it.

Then we shall hate sin as God hates it, and love the soul as God loves it. For these words that God spoke are an endless comfort: 'I will hold you securely.'

CHAPTER 40

After this, our Lord taught me about prayer. In this Showing there are two parts of our Lord's teaching: one is rightful prayer, and the other is trust.

Yet often we do not trust him completely, for we are not sure that God hears us, because we are unworthy – it seems to us – and because we feel absolutely nothing. For often we are as dry and barren after our prayers as we were before. And feeling like this, in our folly, is the cause of our weakness – for I have felt like this myself.

And our Lord brought all this suddenly into my mind and spoke these words and said:

'I am the ground of your praying. First, it is my will that you should have this. Then I make it your will, too. Then I make you ask for it, and you ask. How then should you not have what you pray for?'

In the first words: 'And you ask', he shows the great pleasure and endless reward he will give us for our prayers.

The second words: 'How then should you not have . . . etc.', were said to show an impossibility. For it is quite impossible that we should pray for mercy and grace and not receive it.

For everything our good Lord makes us pray for, he has ordained that we should have since before time began.

CHAPTER 41

B y this we can see that God's goodness is not caused by our praying. He showed this clearly in the sweet words he spoke when he said: 'I am the ground . . .'

And it is our Lord's will that those on earth who love him should know this – and that the more we know, the more we should pray (if it is wisely done). And this is our Lord's meaning.

Prayer is the new, gracious, lasting will of the soul, joined and fastened into the will of our Lord, through the deep inward working of the Holy Spirit.

Our Lord himself is the first to receive our prayer, as I see it. He takes it, full of thanks and joy, and he sends it up above and sets it in the treasury, where it will never be lost. It is there before God, with all his holy ones – continually heard, continually helping our needs. When we come to heaven, our prayers will be given to us as part of our delight – with endless, joyful thanks from God.

Our prayer makes God glad and happy. He wants it and waits for it so that, by his grace, he can make us as like him in condition as we are by creation. This is his blessed will.

CHAPTER 41

So he says this: 'Pray inwardly, even though you find no joy in it. For it does good, even though you feel nothing, see nothing – yes, even though you think you cannot pray. When you are dry and empty, sick and weak, your prayers please me – though there be little enough to please you. All believing prayer is precious to me.'

Because of the reward and endless thanks he longs to give us in return, he is avid for our prayers continually. God accepts the goodwill and work of his servants, no matter how we feel.

Our work of prayer and our work of living well – which we do by his grace – both please him. We must direct our strength through him until the time when we have what we seek – that is, Jesus, in the fullness of joy.

CHAPTER 41

Thankfulness and prayer belong together. Thanking is the deep inward certainty that moves us to reverence and loving awe, so that we turn all our strength to the work that God shows us – giving praise and thanks in the depths of our hearts.

Sometimes thanksgiving overflows into words and says: 'Good Lord, I thank you. Blessed be your name.'

And sometimes, when our hearts are dry and cannot feel, or when we are surrounded by temptation, then we are driven by reason and grace to call upon our Lord with our voice, recalling his blessed Passion and great goodness.

And the virtue of the Lord's word enters into the soul, and brings our heart to life and leads it, by grace, to true understanding – and makes it pray joyfully, and enjoy our Lord truly.

This is a blessed thanksgiving in his sight.

CHAPTER 41

It is our Lord's will that we should have true understanding, particularly about three things concerning prayer.

The first essential is to know from whom, and how, our prayers spring.

He shows from whom when he says: 'I am the ground . . .'
And he shows how when he says: 'First, it is my will . . .'

The second thing we must know is this: how, and in what way, we should use our prayers. The answer is that our will should become the same as the will of our Lord – and should rejoice in it. This is what he means when he says: 'And I make it your will, too.'

The third thing is that we should know the fruit and outcome of our prayers – that is, to be joined with our Lord and be like him in all things.

For this is the reason and purpose of this lovely Showing. And he will help us, and we shall make his promises come true – blessed may he be!

CHAPTER 42

For this is our Lord's will – that our prayer and our trust should be as great as each other. For if our trust is not as ample as our prayer, we cannot worship God and we hinder and harm ourselves.

And the cause is, as I believe, that we do not know that our Lord is the ground from which our prayers spring, and also that we do not know that prayer is given to us by the grace of his love.

For if we knew this, it would make us trust to have (by our Lord's gift) all that we ask.

For I am sure that no one can ask for mercy and grace with his whole heart unless mercy and grace have already been given to him.

CHAPTER 42

Sometimes it seems that we have been praying a long time, and still do not have what we ask. But we should not be sad. I am sure that what our Lord means is that either we should wait for a better time, or more grace, or a better gift. He wills that we trust him, and understand him, and know that he is Life. And he wills that our understanding is rooted in this with all our strength, and will, and reason, so that this ground becomes our home and dwelling-place.

And he wills that we should understand the following things by the gracious light he gives us:

The first is the way we were created – noble and excellent.

The second is the dear and precious way we were bought again.

The third is that he has made everything beneath us to serve us – and that he looks after it for love of us.

So he means this, as if he said: 'Look and see. I have done all this before you ever said a prayer – and now you are made and can pray to me.'

CHAPTER 42

He means by this, that we ought to know that the greatest deeds have already been done, as holy church teaches.

And in thinking this with thankful hearts, we ought to pray for the deed that is being done now – and that is, that he governs and guides us to worship him in this life and to bring us to his joy. For this is the reason he has done all the rest.

This is his meaning – that we should see what he does and pray that it should be done. One is not enough without the other.

For if we pray and do not see what he is doing, then it makes us sad and full of doubts – and that is no praise to him.

And if we see his work and do not pray, then we fail in our duty. And it does no good – that is to say, he does not recognise it.

But when we see his work and pray that it shall be done – this honours him and helps us.

CHAPTER 42

It is our Lord's will that, whatever he plans to do, we should pray for it, either in particular or in general. The joy and delight it gives him – and the thanks and glory that we shall be given because of it – pass all understanding, as I see it.

For prayer is the proper understanding of the fullness of joy that is to come – with deep desire and sure trust.

Lack of the joy we were created to have fills us with deep desire. True understanding and love (with dear remembrance of our Saviour) makes us trust, by his grace.

Our Lord looks on us continually as we work at these two – for we owe it to him, and his goodness expects no less from us. And when we have done so we shall count it nothing – as it is.

If we do what we can, and ask in truth for mercy and grace, then all we lack we shall find in him. And this is what he means when he says: 'I am the ground of your praying.'

And so, by these blessed words and by this Showing, I saw that all our weaknesses and all our doubts and fears shall be overcome.

CHAPTER 42

Prayer joins the soul to God. For though the soul, restored by grace, is always like God in its nature and substance, it is often unlike God in its condition, because of man's sin.

Then prayer is a witness that the soul's will is the same as God's will. And it comforts our conscience and helps us to grace. And so he teaches us to pray, and firmly to trust that we shall have what we pray for.

For he looks on us with love, and wants to make us his partner in good deeds. And so he leads us to pray for what it is his pleasure to do. And he will reward us, and give us endless recompense for these prayers and our goodwill – which are his gifts to us. And this was shown in the words: 'And you ask.'

In these words, God showed such pleasure and such great delight, as if he were in our debt for every good deed that we do. And yet it is he who does them.

And because we ask him eagerly to do the things he loves to do, it is as if he said: 'What could please me better than to ask me – eagerly, wisely, and willingly – to do the very thing I am about to do?' And so, by prayer the soul is attuned to God.

CHAPTER 43

When, by his grace, our courteous Lord shows himself to our soul, then we have all we desire. And, for the time being, we see nothing left to pray for, but all our mind and strength is gathered up in the sight of him. This is a high, unimaginable prayer, in my sight.

For all the reasons why we pray are gathered together in looking upon, and seeing, him to whom we pray – rejoicing wonderingly with reverent fear, and with such great joy and delight in him that for a time we are not able to pray for anything except what he leads us to ask.

And I know full well that the more a soul sees of God, the more it desires him, by his grace.

But when we cannot see him like this, then we have need and cause to pray, because of our failures, to bring ourselves closer to Jesus.

When the soul is tempest-tossed, troubled, and cut off by worries, then is the time to pray – so as to make the soul more responsive towards God. But there is no kind of prayer that can make God more responsive to the soul, for God is always constant in love.

CHAPTER 43

I saw that, whenever we feel the need to pray, our good Lord follows us, helping our desire.

And when, by his special grace, we behold him clearly, knowing no other need, then we follow him and he draws us towards himself by love. For I saw and understood that his great overflowing love brings all our gifts to fulfilment.

I saw, too, that his unceasing work in everything is done so well, so wisely, and so mightily, that it is beyond our power to imagine, or guess, or think.

Then there is nothing more for us to do but to look on him with delight, with a great desire to be made one with him, to be centred in his dwelling-place, and to rejoice in his love, and delight in his goodness.

Then, by his sweet grace and our own humble, constant prayers, we shall be joined to him now in this life by many secret glimpses of precious inward sights and feelings, which he will measure out to us as we, in our simplicity, can bear.

CHAPTER 43

This is brought about – and shall be – by the grace of the Holy Spirit, and shall continue until the time when we die, still loving God and longing for him.

At that day we shall come to God, knowing ourselves clearly, having God wholly. We shall be enfolded in God for ever, seeing him truly, feeling him fully, hearing him spiritually, smelling him delectably, and tasting him sweetly. And we shall see God face to face, humbly and wholly.

Man, who is made, shall see and look for ever upon God, who is the Maker. No man may see God face to face and go on living – that is to say, in this mortal life.

But when it is God's will, by his special grace, to show himself here on earth, he strengthens man above his nature and limits the Showing, as he thinks fit, to what is profitable for us at the time.

CHAPTER 43

In all the revelations, God often showed that man is always working His will and always giving Him glory unstintingly. And the way this is done was shown in the first Showing, and in a wonderful place – for it was shown in wisdom and truth at work in the soul of our blessed Lady, St Mary. And I hope, by the grace of the Holy Spirit, I shall tell how I saw it.

Truth sees God, wisdom perceives God, and from these two comes a third – holy wondering delight in God, which is love. Where there is truth and wisdom, there is also true love, springing from them both. And it is all of God's making.

For he is endless sovereign truth, endless sovereign wisdom, and endless sovereign love, all which is uncreated. And man's soul is a creature within God and has the same properties – except they have been created.

And so it always does what it was made to do: it sees God, it perceives God, and it loves God.

And so God rejoices in what-is-made, and what-is-made rejoices in God, marvelling at him for ever. And in this marvelling the soul sees God, his Lord and Maker – so high, so great and so good compared with what-is-made that those who have been created think themselves nothing.

But the clearness and cleanness of truth and wisdom make him see and know that he was made for love – and that God looks after him in this love for ever.

CHAPTER 44

God judges us by our true inner nature, which is always kept whole in him, safe and sound for ever. And this judgement comes from his rightfulness.

But men judge us by our outward, changeable nature. This seems now one thing, now another, as it runs after first this and then that. And all this shows outwardly.

The judgement of men is a mixture. Sometimes it is kind and generous, and sometimes it is hard and carping. When it is kind and generous it springs from rightfulness, and when it is hard and carping our good Lord re-makes it, through mercy and grace, and by virtue of his Passion, and so turns it into rightfulness again.

And although these two kinds of judgement are reconciled and run together, yet both of them shall be known in heaven without end.

The first judgement, which springs from God's rightfulness – that is, of his high endless love – is the good and lovely judgement that I saw in all the wonderful revelations, where I saw him assign no whit of blame to us.

But although this was sweet and lovely, yet I could not be fully at peace simply by looking on it. And this was because of the judgement of holy church, which I had learnt beforehand, and which was always in my mind.

CHAPTER 45

Because of the church's judgement, I understood that I must recognise myself as a sinner – and I also understood, by the same judgement, that sinners sometimes deserve anger and blame. But I could not see anger or blame in God. And because of this I had a longing that was greater than I am either able or allowed to tell.

For God himself showed me the higher judgement at that time – and therefore I must needs accept it. And the lower judgement was taught me by holy church – and therefore there was no way in which I could forsake the lower judgement.

And to all this I had no direct answer, but simply a wonderful example of a lord and a servant. And I still stand in longing, and shall until I die, to understand – by grace – these two judgements as I ought to.

For the better understanding we can have of these two judgements, by the gracious leading of the Holy Spirit, the better we shall know and understand our own failings. And the more we see our failings, the more our nature will long – by grace – to be brought to fulfilment in endless joy and bliss.

For this is the reason we were made, and our true inner nature is joyful in God now. And it has been since it was made. And it shall be without end.

CHAPTER 45

But in this fleeting life, here in our bodies, we cannot know what our self is, except through faith. But we shall know it – we shall see and know, truly and clearly, what our self is – when we see our God, truly and clearly, in the fullness of joy.

We are able to know ourselves, here in this life, by the continuous help and strength of our high inner nature. And we are able to increase and grow in this knowledge by the help and aid of mercy and grace.

But we can never fully know ourselves until the last point in time. At that point this fleeting life shall come to an end – and so shall all our pain and woe.

And so it is proper for us, by nature and grace, to long and yearn with all our strength to know ourselves. For in this knowledge we shall truly and clearly know our God, in the fullness of joy.

CHAPTER 46

Now during all this time, from beginning to end, I had two different kinds of understanding. One was the endless, continuing love, with its assurance of safekeeping and salvation – for this was the message of all the Showings.

The other was the day-to-day teaching of holy church, in which I had been taught and grounded beforehand, and which I understood and practised with all my heart.

And so in all these Showings it seemed to me that it was right and proper for us to see and know that we are sinners, and do many evil deeds we ought not to do, and leave many good deeds undone that we ought to do – and that we deserve to incur pain and anger because of this.

And, notwithstanding all this, I saw truly that our Lord was never angry, nor ever shall be, for he is God.

He is goodness, life, truth, love and peace. His love and his wholeness cannot allow him to be angry. For I saw truly that it is against the nature of his strength to be angry, and against the nature of his wisdom, and against the nature of his goodness.

God is the goodness that can know no anger, for he is nothing but goodness. Our soul is joined to him – unchangeable goodness – and there is neither anger nor forgiveness between our soul and God, in his sight.

CHAPTER 46

And my soul was led by love and drawn by strength to understand this in every Showing. Our good Lord showed that it is so. And he showed, in truth, that it is so through his great goodness. And he wills that we should long to understand it – that is, in so far as created things are able to understand it.

For it is God's will that the simple soul may be shown – and should know – everything it is able to understand. As for the things it is his will to keep secret, he himself – wisely and powerfully – hides them, for love.

For I saw in the same Showing that many secrets are hidden, which can never be known until God, in his goodness, has made us worthy to see them.

And so I am well content, abiding our Lord's time in this high wonder. And here in this life I trust myself to my mother, holy church, as a simple child should.

CHAPTER 46

Our soul has a duty to do two things. One is to marvel with awe, and the other is to obey humbly, always rejoicing in God. For it is his will that we know that, in a little while, we shall see plainly in him all that we long for.

And in spite of all this, I saw and wondered greatly: 'What is the mercy and forgiveness of God?'

For, by the teaching I had beforehand, I understood that the mercy of God should be the remission of his anger which our sin had caused. For I thought that the anger of God was worse than any other pain for a soul whose intention and desire is to love. And so I thought that the remission of his anger should be one of the main points of his mercy.

But in spite of all my longing and looking I could not see this in all the Showings.

I understood that man is changeable in this life and falls into sin. And the cause of this is blindness, because he does not see God. For if he saw God continually, he would have no wicked feelings, and he would not be led by the longing that leads into sin.

CHAPTER 47

I felt five distinct emotions: rejoicing, sorrow, desire, fear, and sure hope.

Rejoicing: because God let me understand that it was he himself I saw.

Sorrow: because of our failings.

Desire: because I knew and understood that we shall never have full rest until we see him truly and clearly in heaven.

Fear: because it seemed to me that the sight might fade and I should be left on my own.

Sure hope: because I saw that, through his endless love, I should be kept safe by his mercy and brought to his bliss.

And the rejoicing in the sight of him, together with the sure hope of his merciful safekeeping, gave me so much comfort that the fear and sorrow were not too painful.

And yet I saw that this sort of sight of him cannot be continuous in this life, and soon we are thrown back upon ourselves and the contradictions that are within us.

These contradictions spring from the old root of our first sin. And because of this we are tempest-tossed by all manner of pains – both bodily and spiritual – in this life.

CHAPTER 47

But our good Lord the Holy Ghost, who is endless life living in our soul, looks after us safely. He puts peace in our soul and gives it ease, through grace. He attunes it to God and makes it willing. And this is the work of mercy, and the way our Lord continually leads us the whole time we are here in this changing life.

For I saw no anger, except on man's part, and God forgives this anger in us. For anger is no more than a perversity and striving against peace and love. And it is caused either by lack of strength, or lack of wisdom, or lack of goodness. This lack is not found in God, but in us.

For we, because of sin and earthly wretchedness, have anger within us and a continuous striving against peace and love. And he showed he recognised this, many times, by the lovely look of compassion and pity in his face.

And, as much as we fail, so far do we fall. And as far as we fall, so much do we die. For we needs must die, as much as we lose the sight and perception of God, who is our life.

Our failing is full of fear. Our falling is full of shame. And our dying is full of sorrow. But in all this, the sweet eye of pity and love never looks away from us, nor does the working of mercy ever cease.

CHAPTER 48

For I saw a property of mercy, and I saw a property of grace – which have two ways of working in one love. Mercy has a property of pity like a mother's tender love. And grace has a property of glory like the royal lordship of the same love. Mercy works – protecting, enduring, bringing life and healing. And all this comes from the tenderness of love.

And grace works – raising up, rewarding and endlessly outstripping all that our loving and our labour deserve – spreading abroad and showing the high, huge wholeness of God's royal lordship, in his wonderful courtesy. And this is the abundance of love.

For grace turns our fearful failing into overflowing, endless comfort. And grace turns our shameful falling into high, glorious rising. And grace turns our sorrowful dying into holy, blessed life.

For I saw full surely that, just as our mixed contrary feelings bring us pain, shame and sorrow here on earth, even so, by contrast, grace brings us comfort, glory and joy in heaven. And it does so in such abundance that, when we come up to heaven and receive the sweet reward that grace has given us, we shall thank and bless our Lord, and rejoice without end that ever we suffered sorrow.

And then we shall see a property of blessed love in God which we could never have known if we had not first suffered sorrow.

And when I saw all this, I needs must grant that the purpose of God's mercy and his forgiveness is to lessen and quench our anger.

CHAPTER 48

For this was a high marvel to the soul, and it was shown continuously in all the Showings, and I looked on it carefully.

It was shown that, of his nature, our Lord God cannot forgive, for he cannot be angry. It would be impossible.

For this was shown: that our life is rooted and grounded in love, and that without love we cannot live. And so to the soul who by his special grace sees this much of the high marvellous goodness of God – and that we are for ever joined and one with him in love – it is absolutely impossible that God should be angry.

For anger and friendship are two opposites. And so it follows that he who quenches and ends our anger and makes us humble and gentle must always be wholly love, gentle and kind – which is the opposite of anger.

For I saw full surely that, wherever our Lord appears, peace reigns and anger has no place. For I saw no whit of anger in God – in short or long term. For truly, as I see it, if God could be angry, even a little, we should never have life, or place, or being.

For as surely as we owe our being to the endless strength of God, to his endless wisdom and his endless goodness – just as surely we owe our safekeeping to the endless strength of God, his endless wisdom and his endless goodness. For though we poor creatures feel debates and strife within ourselves, yet we are all mercifully enfolded in the gentleness of God – in his kindness, his benignity, in his goodwill.

CHAPTER 49

For I saw full surely that our endless friendship, our dwelling-place, our life and our being are all in God. For the same unending goodness that looks after us while we sin – so we do not perish – is the same unending goodness that continually makes peace between ourselves and our own anger and strife.

This makes us see the need to beseech God, with true reverence, to forgive us and, through grace, to ask him for salvation. For we cannot be blessedly saved until we are truly in peace and love. For that is our salvation.

And though, because of the anger and contradictions within us, we are now in trouble, sadness and woe – as happens to those who are blind and stumble – we are still kept safe and sound by the merciful safekeeping of God, so that we do not perish.

But we cannot know the blessed security of our endless joy until we are filled with peace and love – that is to say, wholly pleased with God, and with all his works, and with all his judgements – and until we are in love and peace with ourselves and with our fellow-Christians, and with all that God loves, as love would have it be. And God's goodness in us brings this about.

CHAPTER 49

So I saw that God is our true peace. He watches over us continually when we can find no rest, and he works continually to bring us to peace that shall never end.

And when, by the power of mercy and grace, we are made humble and gentle, we are wholly safe. Then suddenly the soul is at one with God, when it is truly at peace with itself, for no anger is found in him.

And so I saw that, when we are full of peace and love, we find no contradictions in ourselves, and are not hindered by the contradictions that are in us now. Our Lord in his goodness makes it profitable to us, because these contradictory feelings are the cause of all our troubles and all our sorrow.

And our Lord takes them and sends them up to heaven where they are made more sweet and delectable than heart can think, or tongue can tell. And when we get there we shall find them waiting, all turned into lovely and lasting glory.

So God is our sure rock, and he shall be our whole joy and make us changeless as he is when we reach heaven.

CHAPTER 49

And in this mortal life, mercy and forgiveness are the pathway that always leads us to grace. And because of the storms and sorrows that befall us we often seem dead, as men judge on earth. But in God's sight the soul that shall be saved was never dead, and never shall be.

But at this I wondered and was amazed with all the strength of my soul and thought this: 'Good Lord, I see that you are truth itself, and I know truly that we sin grievously all the day long and are much to blame. And I can neither forsake knowing this truth, nor do I see you put any blame on us. How can this be?'

For I knew by the daily teaching of holy church, and by my own feelings, that the blame for our sin hangs heavy upon us, from the first man until the time we come up to heaven. This, then, was my wonder – that I saw our Lord putting no more blame upon us than if we were as clean and as holy as the angels in heaven.

And my mind was greatly troubled in its blindness, by these two contradictions. And I knew no rest, for fear that his blessed presence should pass from my sight and I should be left not knowing how he looks on us in our sin.

For either I needed to see in God that all sin was done away with, or else I needed to see in God how he regards it – so that I should know truly how I should look on sin and the nature of our blame.

CHAPTER 50

My longing lasted as I looked on him continually, and still I could have no peace because of the fear and perplexity I was in. For I thought: 'If I take it that we are not sinners and deserve no blame, it seems that I should err and not know the truth. And if it is true that we are sinners and deserve blame, good Lord, how can it be that I cannot see this truth in you, who are God, my Maker, in whom I long to see all truth?'

'Three things make me bold to ask. The first is that it is so low a thing – for if it were a high thing I should be afraid to ask. The second is that it is so commonplace – for if it were special and secret I should be afraid, too. The third is that I need to know it, it seems to me, if I am to live here on earth, so that I can know good and evil and – through grace and reason – distinguish between them. Then I can love good and hate evil, as holy church teaches.'

I cried inwardly with all my strength, reaching into God for help, meaning this: 'Ah, Lord Jesus, king of bliss, how shall I have peace? Who shall teach me and tell me what I need to know, if I cannot see it in you now?'

CHAPTER 50

Then our courteous Lord answered by showing, very mistily, a wonderful example of a lord who has a servant, and let me see a double meaning in them both.

The first meaning I saw was this: I saw two actual people, a lord and a servant. And God let me understand them spiritually.

The lord sits with dignity, at rest and in peace. The servant stands reverently by before his lord, ready to do his will. The lord looks upon his servant lovingly and tenderly, and gently sends him to a certain place to do his bidding.

The servant does not simply go, but leaps up and runs off at great speed to do his bidding, because he loves his lord. And then he falls into a gully and is very badly hurt. And then he groans and moans, and wails and writhes, but he cannot get up or help himself at all.

And in all this, the worst thing I saw befall him was that he had no comfort. For he could not turn his head to look upon his loving lord, who was near him and from whom all comfort flows.

And I looked carefully to see any blame or fault in him, or if his lord should lay any blame upon him, and truly there was none to be seen. For the only reason he fell was because of his goodwill and his great desire – and he was still as eager and good at heart after he fell as he was when he stood before his lord, ready to do his bidding.

CHAPTER 51

Then the courteous lord said this: 'Behold my much-loved servant, what harm and hurt has he got in my service for love of me – yes, and all because of his goodwill. Is it not right and proper that I should repay him for his fear and his fright, his hurt and his harm, and all his sorrow? And, more than this, does it not fall to me to give him a gift that is better and more honour to him than his own lack of harm would have been? It seems to me I should do him no favour if I did less.'

And at this point, the sight of the actual example vanished and our Lord himself led on my mind, in seeing and understanding, until the end of this revelation. But, in spite of all the prompting God gave me, the example still perplexed me. For I thought it had been given me to answer my question (whether God blames us for our sin) and yet I could not understand it well enough for it to give me any comfort at that time.

But twenty years after the time of the Showing, all but three months, I was taught inwardly – as I shall set down:

'You must pay close heed to all the circumstances and details that were shown in the example, even though it seems to you they were obscure and unimportant.'

CHAPTER 51

I began by looking at the lord and the servant, and the way the lord sat, and the place where he sat, the colour of his clothes and their shape, and his outward appearance, and at his nobleness and goodness within. I looked at the way the servant stood, and where and how he stood, at the way he was dressed, the colour and shape of his clothes, at his outward appearance and at his inward goodness and eagerness.

The lord who sat in solemn state, at rest and in peace, I understand is God. The servant who stood before the lord I understand was meant as Adam – that is to say, one man was shown then, and his fall, to make it plain from this how God regards a man and his fall. For in the sight of God all men are one man, and one man is all men.

This man was hurt in his body and made weak, and he was stunned in his mind, because he turned away from looking towards God. But his will was kept whole in God's sight. For I saw our Lord commend and approve his will, even though the man himself was held back, and was so blinded that he did not know what his own will was.

And this was the beginning of the teaching I had at that time, through which I was able to come to know how he looks upon us in our sin.

And then I saw that it is only pain itself that hurts and grieves us, and that our courteous Lord comforts us and grieves over us. He always looks upon the soul with gladness, loving us, and longing to bring us back into his bliss.

CHAPTER 51

The place where the lord sat was simple, on barren earth, alone in the wilderness. His clothes were wide and flowing, as befits a lord. The colour of his clothes was blue as azure, sober and lovely. His look was merciful. The colour of his face was a light brown, with handsome features. His eyes were black, beautiful and seemly, with a look of lovely pity. Within him was a great court, long and broad, all full of endless heavens.

His sitting on the bare and desert earth is to mean this: he made man's soul to be his own city and dwelling-place, and man's soul is the most pleasing to him of all his works. But while man had fallen into sorrow and pain, he was not fit to be his city.

And so our own Father would not choose himself another place, but sits on the earth waiting for mankind, who was made from earth, until such time as his dear Son, with hard labour, has brought his city back to noble beauty again.

The blueness of the clothes shows steadfastness. The brownness of his fair face, with seemly blackness of the eyes, was to show his holy dignity. The ampleness of his clothes, which were lovely, flowing around him, shows that he has enfolded in himself all the heavens, and all joy and bliss.

CHAPTER 51

And still I wondered, seeing the lord and the servant, as I said before. I saw the lord sit in state, and the servant standing reverently before his lord. There is a twofold meaning in his servant – one outward, the other inward.

Outwardly, he was clad simply as a labourer in his working clothes. And he stood very close to the lord – not directly in front of him but partly to the side, the left side. He was dressed in a white shirt, just one garment, old and shabby, stained with the sweat of his body, narrow-fitting and short – about a hand's breadth below the knee – threadbare and looking as if it was nearly worn out, just about to fall into rags and tatters.

And at this I greatly wondered, thinking: 'These are most unseemly clothes for a servant who is so much loved to wear before so great a lord.'

For it seemed by the outward look of his clothes that he had been a constant labourer for a long time. But by the inward sight that I had of both the lord and the servant it seemed he was a new servant – a servant who had never been sent out before.

CHAPTER 51

There was a treasure in the earth which the lord loved. I marvelled and wondered what it could be. And I was answered in my mind: 'It is a food which is sweet and pleasant to the lord.'

For I saw the lord sit as a man, and yet I saw neither meat nor drink that could be given him. This was one wonder. Another wonder was that this great lord had only one servant, and he sent him out on an errand. I looked at this, wondering what sort of work it might be that the servant had to do.

And then I understood that he should undertake the greatest labour and the hardest toil there is – he should be a gardener. He should dig and delve, toil and sweat, and turn the earth over and dig into the depths of it, and water the plants in season.

And he should carry on his work in this and make sweet streams flow, and noble and plentiful fruit to spring forth, which he could bring to his lord and give him for his delight. And he should never turn again until he had prepared this food perfectly, as he knew it pleased his lord.

The servant stands for the Son, the second person of the Trinity. And the servant also stands for Adam, that is to say, all men.

CHAPTER 51

When Adam fell, God's son fell. For the holy joining which was made in heaven means that God's son could not be separated from Adam, and by Adam I mean all men. Adam fell from life to death in the pit of this miserable world, and after that he fell into hell.

God's son fell, with Adam, into the depths of the Virgin's womb – who was Adam's fairest daughter. And he did it to take away Adam's blame, both in heaven and on earth – and with great power he fetched him back from hell.

And by this our good Lord Jesus has taken all our blame upon him – and therefore the Father neither can, nor wants to, put any more blame upon us than upon his own Son, beloved Christ.

And so Christ was the servant before he came into the world, standing waiting before the Father, at his command, until the time God willed to send him out to do that glorious Deed by which mankind was brought back again to heaven.

And then he set off eagerly at his Father's command, taking no thought for himself and his great pain, and at once he fell low into the Virgin's womb. The white shirt is the flesh; that he had just one garment shows there is nothing between godhead and manhood; the narrowness is poverty; the age comes from Adam's wearing it; the sweat stains are from Adam's labour; the shortness shows the servant's hard work.

And so I saw the Son stand there, saying in his heart: 'Lo, my dear Father. I stand before you in Adam's shirt, all ready to set off and run. I will gladly be on earth to work to your glory when it is your will to send me. How long shall I wait in longing?'

CHAPTER 51

Also in this wonderful example I have a key of learning – as it were the beginning of an ABC – by which I can have some understanding of our Lord's meaning.

The fact that the Father is sitting shows his godhead, that is to say, in showing him at rest and in peace – for there can be no labour in the godhead. And when he showed himself as a lord, it is a sign of our manhood.

The fact that the servant stands is a sign of work; to the side and on the left shows that he is not worthy to stand directly in front of the lord. His setting off was the godhead, and the running was the manhood. For the godhead springs from the Father into the Virgin's womb, and falls to take our nature upon him. In this falling he took great hurt. The hurt that he took was our flesh, in which he had to bear the agony of the pains of death.

The fact that he stood reverently before his lord, and not even straight in front of him, shows that his clothes were not good enough to stand directly in front of the lord, and that it neither could, nor should, be his place to stand there while he was a labourer.

It also showed that he might not sit in rest and peace with his lord until he had earned his peace, rightfully, with his own hard work. That he was at the left side shows that the Father willingly left his own son to be in manhood to suffer all man's pains without sparing him.

The fact that his shirt is just about to fall into rags and tatters shows the whips and lashes, the thorns and the nails, the pulling and the dragging, the tearing of his tender flesh.

CHAPTER 51

His body was in the grave until Easter morning, and from that time he never lay down again. For then the twisting and writhing, the groaning and moaning was rightly at an end.

And our foul mortal flesh that God's son took upon him, which was Adam's old shirt – narrow, threadbare and short – was then made beautiful by our Saviour – white and shining and for ever spotless, richer and more beautiful than the clothes I saw on the Father. For the Father's clothes were blue, but Christ's clothes now are of a glorious, lovely mixture that is so wonderful that I cannot describe it – for it is all bright with honour.

Now the lord no longer sits on bare earth in the wilderness, but he sits on the noblest throne that he has made in heaven for his pleasure. Now the Son no longer stands before the Father in awe as a servant, poorly clad and half naked. But he stands directly in front of the Father, richly dressed in flowing glory with a crown of precious richness on his head.

For it was shown that we are his crown – and that crown is the Father's joy, the Son's glory, the Holy Spirit's delight and the endless wondering joy of all who are in heaven.

Now the Son no longer stands before the Father on the lefthand side like a labourer, but he sits at his Father's right hand in everlasting rest and peace. Now is the bridegroom, God's son, at peace with his beloved wife, who is the fair maid of endless joy. Now the Son, true God and true man, sits in his city of rest and peace, which his Father has prepared for him by his will, which has no end and no beginning. And the Father is in the Son, and the Holy Ghost in the Father and in the Son.

CHAPTER 51

And so I saw that God rejoices that he is our father, and God rejoices that he is our mother, and God rejoices that he is our true husband, and the soul his beloved wife. And Christ rejoices that he is our brother, and Jesus rejoices that he is our saviour.

These are five great joys, as I see it, which he wants us to delight in – praising him, thanking him, loving him and blessing him for ever.

All of us who shall be saved have, during this lifetime, an amazing mixture of good and ill within us. We have within us Jesus, our risen Lord. We have within us the misery of the mischief of Adam's fall and dying.

By Christ we are steadfastly kept safe, and by his touch of grace we are lifted up to sure hope of salvation. By Adam's fall we are so fragmented in our feelings in so many ways – by sins, and sundry pains – that we are in the dark, and so blind we can scarcely know any comfort.

But in our inward will we wait upon God and faithfully trust to have mercy and grace. And this is his own work in us. And in his goodness he opens the eye of our understanding and gives us sight – sometimes more and sometimes less, as God makes us able to understand it.

And now we are lifted up to one, and now we are allowed to fall into the other.

CHAPTER 52

This is such an amazing mixture in us that we scarcely know how we or our fellow-Christians stand because of these astonishing mixed feelings. But the same holy will, which we give to God when we perceive him, is always truly willing to be with him – with all our heart and strength. And so then we hate and despise our evil promptings and everything that could be the occasion for sin – both spiritual and bodily.

But even so, when this goodness is hidden we are once more blind, and so have sorrow and troubles of all sorts.

But this then is our comfort: that we know in our faith, by virtue of Jesus who safeguards us, that we never give our will to them. But we rail against them, enduring pain and sorrow, and praying, until the time comes when he shows himself to us once again.

And so we live in these mixed feelings all the days of our life.

But his will is that we trust he is always with us, in three ways:

He is with us in heaven, true man in his own person, drawing us up towards him. This was shown by the spiritual thirst.

And he is with us on earth, leading us. And that was shown in the third Showing, where I saw God in a point.

And he is with us endlessly living in our soul, guiding us and guarding us, and this was shown in the sixteenth Showing, as I shall tell.

CHAPTER 52

And so in the servant was shown the mischief and blindness of Adam's fall. And in the servant was also shown the wisdom and goodness of God's Son.

And in the lord was shown the compassion and pity for Adam's woe. And in the lord was also shown the high virtue and endless glory that mankind has come to by virtue of the Passion and death of his much-loved Son.

And so he rejoices greatly at Adam's falling because of the high uplifting and fullness of joy that man is brought to by it – which goes far beyond what we should have had if we had not fallen.

And, so that I should understand this overwhelming glory, my mind was led into the lord at just the moment when I saw the servant fall.

And so now we have matter for mourning, because our sin is the cause of Christ's pain. And we have lasting cause to rejoice, because endless love made him suffer.

And so the man who sees and senses the working of love through grace, hates nothing but sin. For, of all things, as I see it, love and hate are the hardest and most immeasurable opposites.

And, notwithstanding all this, I saw and understood our Lord's meaning that, in this life, we cannot keep ourselves as wholly from sin, in perfect purity as we shall be in heaven. But we may well, by grace, guard against the sins that shall lead to everlasting torment – as holy church teaches – and avoid the pardonable ones, reasonably, as far as we can.

CHAPTER 52

And if we in our blindness and weakness should at any time fall, we should quickly get up, knowing the sweet touch of grace, and bend our will to mend our ways as holy church teaches, according to the badness of the sin, and go at once to God in love. Not on the one hand crawling abjectly as if we were in despair, nor, on the other, being over-bold, as though we thought it did not matter. But plainly acknowledging our weakness, knowing we cannot last for the twinkling of an eye without the safekeeping of grace.

We must cling to God reverently and trust in him only. For God sees things in one way and man sees them in another. For it falls to man to accuse himself humbly, and it falls to God, in his own true goodness, to excuse man courteously.

And these two ways of looking on things were shown in the twofold way the lord looked upon the fall of his much-loved servant. One was shown outwardly, humbly and gently, and with great compassion and pity – and the other was of inward endless love.

And this is how our Lord wills we should accuse ourselves – that we should be willing to see our fall and recognise all the harm that comes from it; that we should see and know we can never undo it; and at the same time, we should be willing to truly see and recognise the unending love he has for us, and his overflowing mercy.

CHAPTER 52

To see and recognise these things both together, through grace, is the gentle accusation our Lord asks from us – and he himself causes it to happen.

And this is the lower part of man's life, and it was shown in the outward look.

And in this Showing I saw two parts: one is the pitiful fall of man, and the other is the glorious payment our Lord has made for man.

The second look was shown inwardly, and it was a higher understanding and was at one with the first. For the life and strength we have in the lower part comes from the higher, and it comes down to us by the natural love that is in us, through grace. There is absolutely nothing separating one from the other, for it is all one love. And this blessed love has a twofold way of working in us.

For in the lower part there are pains and passions, pity and compassion, mercy and forgiveness, and other things that are profitable to us. But in the higher part there are none of these. There is just one high love and marvellous joy, and in this marvellous joy all pains are wholly destroyed.

And in all this our good Lord showed not just our excusing, but also the glorious height he shall bring us to – and that he shall turn all our blame to endless glory.

CHAPTER 52

And so I saw that it is his will that we know that he does not take the fall of any one of those who shall be saved any harder than he took the fall of Adam. And we know that he loved Adam endlessly, and looked after him safely in his need – and that now he has blessedly restored him in high unimaginable joys.

For our Lord God is so good, so gentle and so courteous that he can never put any blame upon those who shall endlessly bless and praise him.

And my great longing was partly answered and my great fear was somewhat eased by what I have just set down, by this lovely, gracious Showing of our Lord God. In this Showing I saw and surely understood that in every soul that shall be saved there is a godly will that never assented to sin, nor ever shall. This will is so good that it can never will any evil. But always and for ever it wills good, and does good, in the sight of God.

And our Lord wills that we know this in our Faith and Belief – specifically and truly – that we all have this godly will, entire and safe, in our Lord Jesus Christ. For, because of God's rightfulness, the same human nature that shall reach fulfilment in heaven needs must be so knitted and joined to Christ that there is a substance within it that never can, nor ever shall, be separated from him. And it is through his own goodwill and his endless far-sighted purpose that this is so.

CHAPTER 53

But in spite of this rightful knitting and this endless joining, the redemption and buying back of mankind is still necessary and profitable in everything. It is done for the same reason and for the same purpose as holy church teaches us through our Faith.

For I saw that God never began to love mankind. For just as man is destined to come to endless joy and crown God's delight in his work, so man in God's thought has always been known and loved from without beginning in his almighty plan.

And by the endless assent and full accord of all the Trinity, the Mid-Person, Christ, wished to be both ground and head of this fair nature, from whom we all come, in whom we are all enfolded, to whom we all return. In him we find our whole heaven of everlasting joy – and this is by the foreseeing purpose of the blessed Trinity since before time was.

For before ever he made us, he loved us – and when we were made we loved him. And this love is created from the innate natural goodness of the Holy Spirit, it is strong by reason of the strength of the Father, and wise by means of the wisdom of the Son.

And so man's soul is made by God,
and in the same moment it is joined to God.

CHAPTER 53

And so I understand that man's soul is created out of nothing – that is to say, it is made, but made from nothing that has itself been created – in this way.

When God wished to create man's body he took the clay of the earth, which is matter mingled and mixed from all earthly things, and he made man's body from it. But when he wanted to make man's soul he took no ingredients, but simply made it.

And so created nature is rightfully united to the Maker, who is Substance and Nature uncreated – that is, God.

And from this it comes that there is nothing, and shall be nothing, between God and man's soul. And in this endless love man's soul is kept whole. And in this endless love we are led and looked after by God, and shall never be lost.

For he wills that we know our soul is a life, and this life, through his goodness and grace, shall continue in heaven for ever – loving him, thanking him, and praising him. And just as we shall live without end, even so we have already lived – treasured in God, hidden – known and loved since before time was.

And so he wills that we know that the noblest thing he ever made is mankind, and that the fullest substance and highest virtue is the blessed soul of Christ. And, further, he wills that we know that Christ's dear soul was intricately knitted to him when he was made man. This knot is subtle and so mighty that it is joined fast to God. And by this joining it is made for ever holy.

Furthermore, he wills that we know that all souls who shall be saved, in heaven without end, are joined by this joining and made holy by this holiness.

CHAPTER 53

And because of the great, unending love that God has for all mankind, he makes no difference in love between the blessed soul of Christ and the humblest soul that shall be saved.

For it is easy to believe and trust that the dwelling of the blessed soul of Christ is right high in the glory of God. And truly, as I understand our Lord's meaning, where the blessed soul of Christ is, there is the substance of all the souls that shall be saved by Christ.

Greatly should we rejoice that God dwells in our soul – and much more greatly we should rejoice because our soul dwells in God. Our soul is created to be God's dwelling-place – and the dwelling-place of the soul is God, who is not created.

It is a high understanding to see and know in our hearts that God, who is our Creator, dwells in our soul. And it is a higher understanding still to see and know in our hearts that our soul, which is created, dwells in God's substance – and that it is from this substance, God, that we are what we are.

And I saw no difference between God and our substance but, as it were, all God. And yet my understanding took it that our substance is contained within God. That is to say, that God is God, and our substance is created by God.

CHAPTER 54

For the almighty truth of the Trinity is our Father –
for he made us and keeps us within him.
And the deep wisdom of the Trinity is our mother –
in whom we are all enfolded.
The high goodness of the Trinity is our Lord –
in whom we are enfolded, and he in us.

We are enfolded in the Father
and we are enfolded in the Son
and we are enfolded in the Holy Spirit.
And the Father is enfolded in us
and the Son is enfolded in us
and the Holy Spirit is enfolded in us –
all might, all wisdom, all goodness.
One God. One Lord.

And our Faith is a virtue that comes from our natural substance into our sensual soul, by the Holy Spirit. All our virtues come to us through faith – for without this no one can receive virtue.

For faith is no more than a proper understanding of our being – with true belief and sure trust – that we are in God and God is in us, although we cannot see it.

And this virtue of faith – and all the others that God has ordained for us that are contained within it – works great things in us. For Christ's merciful working is within us and we, by grace, are attuned to him through the gifts and virtues of the Holy Spirit. By this work we are Christ's children, and Christian in living.

CHAPTER 54

And so Christ is our way, leading us surely in his laws. And Christ in his body mightily bears us up to heaven.

For I saw that Christ, having within him all who shall be saved by him, gloriously makes a gift of us to his Father in heaven. And the Father takes this gift with heartfelt thanks and gives it back to his Son, Jesus Christ. This gift and this work is joy to the Father, and bliss to the Son, and delight to the Holy Spirit.

And of all we ought to do, this gives most joy to our Lord – that we rejoice in the joy which the blessed Trinity enjoys in our salvation. And this was shown in the ninth Showing, where more is said about this.

And notwithstanding all our mixed feelings of good and ill, it is God's will that we understand and believe that we are more at home in heaven than on earth.

Our Faith springs from the natural love in our soul, and from the clear light of reason, and from the steadfast memory we are given by God in our first creation.

At the moment when our soul is breathed into our body, when we are made flesh, at that same moment mercy and grace begin to work, taking care of us and safeguarding us with pity and with love. And through this act the Holy Spirit forms in our Faith the hope that we shall come back up again to our own substance, into the power of Christ, grown and brought to fulfilment by the Holy Spirit.

CHAPTER 55

So I understood that our life in the flesh is rooted in nature, and in mercy, and in grace. It is this grounding that enables us to receive the gifts that lead to endless life.

For I saw full surely that our substance is in God. And I also saw that God is in our life in the flesh.

For at the very point our soul is made flesh – at that self-same point is the city of God, ordained for him since before time was. And he comes to this seat and shall never leave it. For God is never parted from the soul in which he dwells joyfully for ever. And this was shown in the sixteenth Showing, where it says: 'The place that Jesus takes in our soul he shall never leave.'

And all the gifts that God can give to those he has created, he has already given to his Son Jesus for us. And he, dwelling within us, has enfolded all these gifts within him until the time when we are fully grown – our soul with our flesh, and our flesh with our soul, one helping the other – until we have been brought to our full stature by the work of nature.

And then, in the ground of nature and by the work of mercy, the Holy Ghost, by grace, breathes into us all those gifts that lead to life without end.

CHAPTER 55

And this is how my understanding was led by God, to see in him that our soul is a created trinity, like the blessed Uncreated Trinity. It is known and loved since before time was, and in its making it is joined to the Maker.

This sight was sweet and wonderful to behold, full of peace and rest, certainty and delight.

And because of the glorious union God made between the soul and the flesh, it follows that mankind has to be redeemed from double death. And this redemption was not possible until the Son, the second person of the Trinity, had taken upon himself the lower part of mankind – which had been joined to the highest in the original creation.

Both these two parts were in Christ – the higher and the lower. And yet this is only one soul.

The higher part was always one with God in peace and perfect joy and bliss. The lower part, which is in the flesh, suffered for the salvation of mankind.

Both these two parts were seen and felt in the eighth Showing, in which my body was filled full of feeling for Christ's Passion, and his death. For, over and above this, I was shown at the same time a subtle feeling and secret inward sight of the higher part – when I could not look up to heaven, as the voice suggested. This was because of that great vision of the inner life. For this inward life is the high substance, that precious part of the soul that is for ever rejoicing in the godhead.

CHAPTER 55

And so I saw full surely that it is easier for us to know God than to know our own soul. For our soul is so deep-rooted in God, and so endlessly treasured, that we cannot come to know it until we first know God, its Maker, to whom it is joined. But, in spite of this, I saw that we must, to be complete, desire wisely and truly to know our own soul. And by this, we are taught to seek it where it is – and that is, in God.

And so, by the guidance – through grace – of the Holy Spirit, we shall come to know both of them at once, no matter whether it is God or our soul that we seek.

God is nearer to us than our own soul, for he is the ground on which our soul stands. He is the medium that keeps the substance and the flesh so closely knit together that they shall never be separated.

For our soul sits in God in true rest. And our soul stands in God in true strength. And our soul, by its nature, is rooted in God in endless love.

And so, if we want to know our soul, and to walk and talk with it, it is absolutely necessary for us to reach into our Lord God, in whom it is enclosed.

CHAPTER 56

And as regards our substance, it may properly be called our soul. And as regards our flesh, it also can properly be called our soul. And this is because of the way they are joined and made one within God.

The glorious city where our Lord Jesus sits is our flesh, in which he is enclosed. And our natural substance is enclosed in Jesus with the blessed soul of Christ, sitting at rest in the godhead.

And I saw for certain that it needs must follow that we should be in longing and in penance up to the time that we are led so deep into God that we really and truly know our own soul.

And I saw for certain that our good Lord leads us into this high depth by the same love in which he made us, and by the same love in which he bought us, by mercy and grace, and through virtue of his blessed Passion.

And, notwithstanding all this, we can never come to the full knowledge of God until we first know our own soul clearly. For until such time as our soul has grown to its full strength, we cannot be completely holy.

That time will come when our flesh, by means of Christ's Passion, is brought up to heaven to join our substance – with all the rewards for our suffering that God shall give us, through mercy and grace.

CHAPTER 56

And I had a partial insight, and it is grounded in nature – that is to say, our reason is grounded in God, who is nature's substance. Mercy and grace spring from this high natural substance and they spread through us, doing all things and completing our joy.

These are our foundations, in which we have our being, our growth, and our fulfilment. For in nature we have our life and our being. And in mercy and grace we have our growth and fulfilment. These are three properties of one goodness, and where one works, all work, in the things which concern us now.

It is God's will that we should understand this, and that we should ask with all our heart and with all our strength to know them better and better until the time we are brought to fulfilment.

For knowing them fully, and seeing them clearly, is the selfsame thing as the endless joy and bliss we shall have in heaven. And God wills that this joy and bliss should be begun here on earth by our knowing his love.

For we cannot profit by our reason alone, unless we also have intention and love. Nor can we be saved simply because we have our natural foundation in God, unless we also know the mercy and grace that come from that foundation.

For from these three – all working together – we receive all the good we have. The first of these is the goodness of human nature. For when we were first made God gave us as much and as great goodness as we could receive in our spiritual nature alone. But in his foreseeing purpose in his endless wisdom he willed that our nature should be twofold.

CHAPTER 56

Concerning our substance, he made us noble, and so rich that we always do his will and bring him honour. And when I say 'we', it means those who shall be saved.

For truly I saw there are those whom he loves and who always do what pleases him, without holding back. And because he has made us very rich and highly noble, a measure of virtue comes into our soul at the time it is joined to our body, by which joining we are made flesh.

And so in substance we are complete, and in our flesh we are lacking. And God will restore and make good this lack by the working of mercy and grace, which flow into us from the very nature of his godhead.

And so it is the nature of his godhead that brings it about that mercy and grace work in us. And it is from the nature of his godhead that we have from him the ability to receive the working of mercy and grace within us.

I saw that our nature is complete in God, and he makes different parts of it flow out of him to work his will. Nature keeps all these safe – and mercy and grace restore them and bring them to fulfilment. And none of these shall perish.

CHAPTER 57

For the higher part of our nature is knit fast to God by its making, and God is knitted to our lower nature in taking our flesh. And so Christ is our two natures joined together.

For the Trinity is comprehended in Christ – in whom our higher nature is rooted and grounded. And Christ has taken our lower nature upon him – and this nature was designed first of all for him.

For I saw full surely that all the works that God has done, or ever shall do, were fully known to him since before the beginning. And he made mankind for love, and for that same love it was his will to be made man.

The next goodness we receive is our Faith, by which we begin to profit. And our Faith comes into our fleshly soul from the high riches of our natural substance. And it is grounded in us, and we in it, through the natural goodness of God, by the work of mercy and grace. And from this comes all the other good by which we are guided and saved.

For the commandments of God are contained in our Faith, and we should understand them in two ways, which are these:

One is his bidding – the things we should love and do.

The other is his forbidding – the things we should hate and turn our backs on. For in these two all our life's work is contained.

CHAPTER 57

Also contained in our Faith are the Seven Sacraments, one following the other in the order that God has ordained them for us, together with all kinds of virtue.

For, by the goodness of God, the same virtues we received in our substance are given to us again by grace, through the work of mercy. These virtues and gifts are treasured up for us in Jesus Christ.

For at the same time that God knitted himself to our flesh in the maiden's womb, he took our fleshly soul. In doing this, because he already had us enfolded in him, he joined it to our substance.

By this joining he became perfect man. For Christ, having knitted to himself each man who shall be saved, is perfect man.

And so our Lady is our mother, and we are enfolded in her and born of her in Christ. For she who is the mother of our Saviour is also the mother of all who shall be saved by our Saviour.

And our Saviour is our true Mother, and we shall be carried within him for ever, and shall never be born out of him.

CHAPTER 57

God the blessed Trinity is everlasting life and, just as he is endless and without beginning, so it was his endless purpose to make mankind. This fair human nature was first prepared for his own Son, the second person of the Trinity.

And when God willed it, with the full accord of the Trinity, he made all of us at once, and knit us and joined us to himself.

And by this joining we are kept as clean and noble as we were when we were first made. It is by virtue of that same precious joining that we love our Maker, and delight in him, praise him, and endlessly rejoice in him. And this is a work that is going on all the time in every soul that shall be saved. And this is the godly will I spoke of before.

And so in our making God all-mighty is our natural father, and God all-wise is our natural mother, together with the love and goodness of the Holy Spirit – and this is all one God, one Lord.

And in the knitting together and the joining he is our own true husband, and we are his beloved wife and his fair maid, and he will never be displeased with his wife.

For he says: 'I love you, and you love me, and our love shall never be sundered.'

CHAPTER 58

I saw the work of the whole blessed Trinity, and in this sight I saw and understood three properties:

the property of fatherhood
the property of motherhood
and the property of lordship
in one God.

From our father all-mighty we have our safekeeping and our joy as concerns our natural substance, which is ours by creation from without beginning.

And from the second person the Son, with his wit and wisdom, we have our safekeeping in the flesh, our restoration and our redemption – for he is our mother, brother and saviour.

And from our good Lord the Holy Spirit we have the return and reward for our life and labour – and this always goes beyond what we can think to ask, by his marvellous courtesy, and through his high, overflowing grace.

For all our life goes by threes:

First we have our being
second we have our growing
and third we have our fulfilment.

The first is nature
the second is mercy
the third is grace.

CHAPTER 58

As for the first, I saw and understood
that the strength of the Trinity is our father
and the deep wisdom of the Trinity is our mother
and the great love of the Trinity is our Lord
and that we have all these in our nature
and in the substance we got when we were made.

And furthermore, I saw that the second person the Son who is our mother in this substance – that same much-loved person – has become our mother in the flesh.

For we are double-made by God – that is to say, in substance and in flesh.

Our substance is the high part which we get from our father, God all-mighty.

And the Son, the second Person of the Trinity, is our Mother in nature when we are created in substance. We are rooted and grounded in him. And he is our Mother in mercy in taking our flesh.

And so it is that our Mother works in many ways for us, and all our separate parts are kept together in him.

CHAPTER 58

For in our mother Christ we profit and grow, and in mercy he remakes and restores us. And by the power of his Passion, his death, and rising again he rejoins us to our own substance.

And grace works with mercy. And this work properly belongs to the third person, the Holy Spirit.

The Holy Spirit works by rewarding and giving:

Rewarding is a gift of trust that he gives to all those who have laboured.

Giving is a work of courtesy which he does freely by grace, and goes beyond all that created man can deserve.

And so in our father, God all-mighty, we have our being. And in our mother of mercy we are remade and restored. Our fragmented lives are knit together and made perfect man. And by giving and yielding ourselves, through grace, to the Holy Spirit we are made whole.

And our substance is in our father, God all-mighty and our substance is in our mother, God all-wise, and our substance is in our Lord the Holy Spirit, God all-goodness.

Our substance is whole in each person of the Trinity, which is one God. But our flesh is only in the second person, Christ Jesus (in whom are also the Father and the Holy Spirit).

And in Jesus, and by Jesus, we are powerfully brought out of hell, and out of the misery of earth – and gloriously brought up into heaven, and blessedly joined to our substance, increased in richness and glory by the power of Christ and by the grace and work of the Holy Spirit.

CHAPTER 58

And we have all this bliss through mercy and grace. And we should never have had or known this bliss unless the property of goodness that is in God had been challenged. For our bliss comes from this.

For wickedness has been allowed to rise to challenge goodness, and the goodness of mercy and grace challenged the wickedness – and turned everything to goodness and glory for all those who shall be saved. For it is the nature of God to overcome evil.

And so Jesus Christ, who does good to overcome evil, is our true mother. We take our lives from him, which is the start of motherhood, together with all the loving care that follows on, without end.

As truly as God is our father, so, just as truly, God is our mother. And he showed this in everything, especially in those sweet words when he said:

'It is I'. That is to say,
'It is I, the strength and goodness of fatherhood.
It is I, the wisdom of motherhood.
It is I, the light and grace of holy love.
It is I, the Trinity.
It is I, the unity.
I am the sovereign goodness in all things.
It is I who teach you to love.
It is I who teach you to desire.
It is I who am the lasting fulfilment of all true desires.'

CHAPTER 59

For the soul is highest, noblest, and worthiest when it is lowest, humblest, and gentlest.

And from the ground of this substance spring all our virtues and our sensibilities – both by the gift of nature, and by the help and aid of mercy and grace.

For without mercy and grace we cannot come to good.

Our high father, God all-mighty, who is life, knew us and loved us since before time was. And knowing us – in his wonderful deep love, and with the far-seeing endless counsel of all the blessed Trinity – he willed that the second person should become our mother, our brother and our saviour.

And it follows from this that, as truly as God is our father so, just as truly, he is our mother.

Our father wills.
Our mother works.
Our good Lord the Holy Spirit sees that it is done.

And so it is right that we should love our God from whom we have our being, and that we should reverently thank and praise him because he made us.

And that we should pray hard to our mother of mercy and pity, and to our good Lord the Holy Spirit, for help and grace.

CHAPTER 59

[134]

For all our life lies in these three:

nature,
mercy
and grace.

And from these come humbleness, gentleness, patience and pity – and the hatred of sin and wickedness. For it is the property of virtues to hate sin and wickedness.

And so Jesus is our true mother in nature, by our first creation. And he is our true mother in grace, by taking our created nature.

All the good work – and all the sweet, kind care of beloved motherhood – are given to the second person. For in him we have this godly will kept whole and safe for ever, both in nature and in grace, by his own proper goodness.

I saw three ways to understand the motherhood of God.

The first is grounded in our natural making.

The second lies in Christ taking that nature – and here begins the motherhood of grace.

The third is the work of motherhood.

And in this begins a pouring forth, by the same grace, of endless length and breadth and height and depth of all his love.

CHAPTER 59

But now I needs must say a little more concerning this outpouring, as I understood it from our Lord's teaching. It tells how we were brought back again, by the motherhood of mercy and grace, into our own proper place – where the motherhood of natural love made us. And this natural love never leaves us.

Our natural mother, our gracious mother – for he willed wholly to become our mother in all things – humbly and gently found the place to begin his work in the maiden's womb. And he showed this in the first Showing, where he brought that gentle maid into my mind's eye, at the tender age she was when she first conceived. That is to say, it was in this humble place that our high God, who is the sovereign wisdom of all, set himself to grow, and clothed himself in our poor flesh so that he himself could undertake the work and care of motherhood in all things.

A mother's care is the closest, nearest and surest – for it is the truest. This care never might, nor could, nor should, be fully done except by him alone. We know our own mother bore us into pain and dying. But our true Mother Jesus, who is all love, bears us into joy and endless living. Blessed may he be!

And so he nourished us within himself for love, and he laboured until the full term, because he willed to suffer the sharpest pangs and deepest pains that ever were or ever shall be. And at the end he died. And when he had done this – and so borne us into bliss – yet even all this could not assuage his marvellous love. And he showed this in those high, wonderful words of love: 'If I could have suffered more, I would have suffered more.'

CHAPTER 60

He could die no more, but he would not cease from working. And so he needs must feed us. For the dear love of motherhood has given him a duty to us. A mother feeds her child with her milk, but our beloved Mother, Jesus, feeds us with himself. He feeds us courteously and tenderly with the Blessed Sacrament – which is the precious food of life itself.

And he nourishes us with all the sweet sacraments, with full mercy and grace. And this is what he meant by that blessed word when he said: 'It is I that holy church preaches and teaches you.' It means this: 'All the healing and life of the sacraments, all the virtue and grace of my word, all the goodness that is set down by holy church for you – it is I.'

A mother can lean her child tenderly on her breast, but our tender mother Jesus can lead us simply into his blessed breast through his dear wounded side. There he will show us a part of the godhead and of the joys of heaven – with inward certainty of endless bliss. He showed this in the tenth Showing, where he gave the same meaning by these dear words when he said 'Look how I loved you' as he looked into his side rejoicing.

This dear and lovely word 'mother' is so sweet, and so true to its nature, that it cannot properly be said of anyone but of him, and of she who is the true mother of him and of us all.

CHAPTER 60

From the nature of motherhood springs natural love, wisdom and understanding – and it is good. For even though our fleshly birth is only little, low and simple compared with our spiritual birth, yet it is he who brings this about in those who are born.

A kind loving mother, who knows and understands the needs of her child, looks after it tenderly as is her way and nature. And as it grows bigger she changes her ways, but not her love. And when it grows older still she allows it to be spanked, to break it from vice and lead it to goodness and grace. And our Lord does the same thing in the same way, truly and well, to those he brings up.

So he is our natural mother, by the work of grace in our lower nature out of love for our higher nature. And it is his will that we know this, for he wants our love to be joined fast to him.

And in all this I saw that the duty we owe our own fathers and mothers, as God commanded us, is fulfilled in truly loving God for his fatherhood and motherhood of us. And it is Christ who brings us to this blessed love.

And this was shown in all the Showings, and especially in the high, overflowing words when he said: 'It is I that you love.'

CHAPTER 60

And at our spiritual birth he shows such loving care that there is nothing to compare it with – because our soul is so much more precious in his sight than anything else.

He fires our understanding, he directs our ways, he comforts our soul, he lightens our heart and gives us – in part – knowledge and love of his blessed godhead – and an understanding, by grace, of his dear manhood and blessed Passion, and humble wonder at his high, overflowing goodness. And he makes us love all that he loves, for love of him, and to be well satisfied by him and all his works.

When we fall, he quickly lifts us up with his loving grip and touch of grace. And when we are thus strengthened by his dear deeds, then we choose him of our own will – through his sweet grace – to be his servants and lovers for ever, without end.

And after this, he allows some of us to fall harder and more painfully than we ever did before, it seems to us. And then we – who do not know everything – think all our work is wasted. But it is not so. We need to fall, and we need to see we have fallen. For if we never fell, we should never know how poor and weak we are on our own – nor should we ever fully know the wonderful love of our Maker.

For in heaven we shall see without end that we have sinned grievously in this life and, in spite of this, we shall see we were never less in his love, nor were we ever less precious in his sight.

And through the trial of this failure we shall have a high, wonderful knowledge of love in God, without end. For it is a strong and wonderful love which cannot, nor will not, be broken because of wrong-doing.

CHAPTER 61

[139]

This is one profitable understanding. Another is the lowliness and humbleness we shall gain from looking on our failure – and because of this we shall be raised high in heaven. And we could never have reached such height without such humbling.

And so we ought to look upon our fall – for if we do not see it, even though we fall, we cannot profit from it. And it usually happens that first we fall, and then we see it – and we do both by the mercy of God.

A mother may sometimes let her child fall and be unhappy in many ways for its own good. But she will never allow any real harm to come to the child, because of the love she bears it. And though an earthly mother may have to allow her child to die, our heavenly mother Jesus will not allow any one of us who is his child to perish. For he is all power, all wisdom and all love – and no one is but he. Blessed may he be!

CHAPTER 61

But often, when our falling and our miserable sin is shown to us, we are so ashamed we scarcely know where to put ourselves. But our loving mother does not want us to run away from him then, for he does not love us less.

But he wills that we behave as children do. For when they are unhappy or frightened they run quickly to their mother for help, with all their might, saying this: 'My own mother, my dear mother, please pity me. I have made myself unclean and unlike you, and I cannot heal myself without your special help and grace.'

And if we do not begin to feel better straight away, we can be sure he is behaving like a wise mother. For if he sees it is better for us to sorrow and weep, he allows us to be sad for a while, pitying us and sorrowing with us, for love.

And he wills that we behave like a child who always trusts its mother's love, both in happiness and sadness, and that we cling strongly to the faith of holy church, so that we find our beloved mother there, in the comfort of true understanding with all the blessed Communion of saints. For one single person may often break down, as it seems to him – but the whole body of holy church has never been broken, nor ever shall be, without end.

In all this, he takes the part of a kind nurse who has no other care but the welfare of her child. It is his office to save us, it is his glory to do it, and it is his will that we should know it.

For it is his will that we should love him dearly, and trust in him humbly and strongly. And he showed this in these gracious words: 'I will hold you securely.'

CHAPTER 61

At this time he showed how frail we are,
and how we fall;
how we are broken and count for nothing;
how we are despised and cast out:
all the sorrows, far and wide, it seemed to me, that we
can suffer in this life.

And at the same time he showed his blessed strength, his blessed wisdom, and his blessed love.

He showed that he looks after us as tenderly and sweetly when we are sorrowful – to his glory and our salvation – as he does when we have most ease and comfort.

And it is by this that he raises us spiritually and highly in heaven, and turns all this to his praise and our joy for ever. For his love never allows us to lose our time.

And all this comes from the natural goodness of God by the work of grace. God, in his being, is nature – that is to say, the goodness that is nature is God.

He is the ground, he is the substance, he is the same thing as nature, and he is the true father and mother of nature.

And all the natures he has made, which flow out of him to work his will, shall be restored and brought back to him again by man's salvation, through the work of grace.

CHAPTER 62

For, of all the natures he has planted in many creatures, to be part of them, man alone has the whole nature in fullness, in virtue, in beauty and in goodness, in royalty and nobility, in all manner of solemnity of worth and worship.

In this we can see that we are wholly bound to God by nature, and we are wholly bound to God by grace.

In this we may see that there is no great need for us to search far and wide to know all different kinds of nature, but simply to seek into holy church, our mother's breast – that is to say, into our own soul, where our Lord dwells.

And there we shall find everything, here in this life, through faith and understanding. And afterwards we shall find it truly in God himself, plainly in paradise.

But let no man or woman think that this whole nature is his alone. It is the same for all of us. This fair nature is our dear Christ, and was made for him, so that the making of man might be noble and glorious – and that man's salvation might be full of joy and bliss.

And he saw, and knew, and understood all this before time began.

CHAPTER 62

In this we can see that we have to hate sin by our very nature – and we have to hate sin by virtue of grace, too. For nature is all good and fair in itself, and grace was sent out to save nature, to destroy sin, and to bring that fair nature back again to the blessed point it came from – that is, God. And to bring it back with more honour and worship than before, by the good work of grace.

For all the holy ones of God shall see before him, in joy without end, that nature has been tried in the fire of tribulation and no fault has been found in it, nothing lacking. And so nature and grace are of one accord – for grace is God, just as nature is God.

He is double in the way he works and one in the way he loves, and neither of them operates without the other, and they shall never be separated.

And when, by God's mercy and with his help, we attune ourselves to nature and grace, we shall truly see that sin is, in truth, viler and more painful than hell – without compare – for it is against our fair nature. For as truly as sin is unclean, just as truly it is unnatural. And so it is a horrible sight for the beloved soul that longs to be all clean and shining in the sight of God – as nature and grace both teach it.

But we must not be frightened by this, except as much as is good for us. We must humbly take our sorrow to our beloved mother, and he will sprinkle us with his precious blood, and make our soul humble and gentle. He will heal us wholly in his good time, as is most glory to him and joy to us, without end.

CHAPTER 63

He shall never cease or lessen this sweet and lovely work until all his beloved children have been born and brought forth. And this was shown when he gave me understanding of the spiritual thirst – that is, the love-longing that shall last until doomsday. And so our life is grounded in our true Mother, Jesus, as he in his far-seeing wisdom saw since before time was – together with the high power of the Father and the high sovereign goodness of the Holy Ghost.

And in taking our nature he gave us life, and in his blessed dying on the cross he bore us to life without end. And from that time, and now, and for ever until Judgement Day, he feeds us and looks after us – as the high sovereign nature of motherhood and the natural need of children demand.

Fair and sweet is our heavenly mother in our soul's sight, and dear and lovely are the gracious children in our heavenly mother's sight – gentle, humble, with all the sweet virtues that belong to children by nature.

For the child by nature does not think its mother does not love it. The child by nature does not rely on itself. The child by nature loves its mother and each of them loves the other. These are lovely virtues, and there are others like them that praise and please our heavenly mother.

And I saw no higher stature in this life than childhood – in its weakness, its small strength and little wit – until the time that our gracious mother has brought us up to our Father's joy. And at that time the meaning of those sweet words shall be made truly clear when he says: 'All shall be well, and you shall see for yourself that all manner of thing shall be well.'

CHAPTER 63

Before this time, I had a great longing and desire to be delivered from the world and from this life, by God's gift – for I saw so often the sorrow that is here and the joy and bliss that is there. And even if there had been no pain in this life except the absence of our Lord, I sometimes thought it was more than I could bear.

And so I began to sorrow and yearn so much that – what with my own misery, idleness and weakness – I had no joy to live and to work as was my lot.

And to all this our courteous Lord answered, and said in these words: 'Suddenly you shall be taken from all your pain, from all your sickness, from all your unhappiness, and from all your sorrow. You shall come up above and you shall have me for your reward. And you shall be filled to the brim with love and happiness.

'And you shall have no more pain, no more unhappiness, no lack of what you long for, but you shall always have joy and bliss without end. Why should it grieve you to suffer a while, seeing it is my will and to my worship?'

CHAPTER 64

In these words, 'Suddenly you shall be taken', I saw that God rewards a man for the patience he shows in waiting upon God's will – and he rewards him for his time, and rewards him because a man has to stretch out his patience over the length of his days, since he does not know when he will die. This is great profit to him. For if a man knew when he was going to die, his patience would not last beyond then.

And God wills that the whole time the soul is in the body it should seem to itself that it is always at the point of being taken. For all this life and all this languishing we have here is but a moment in time – and when we are suddenly taken out of pain into bliss, the pain shall be nothing.

And at this time I saw a body lying on the earth. It looked heavy and ugly, without shape or form – like a swollen swamp of stinking slime. And suddenly a lovely fair creature sprang out of this body – a little child, fully shaped and formed, swift and lively, whiter than a lily – and quickly glided up to heaven.

The grossness of the body shows the great misery of our mortal flesh, and the smallness of the child shows the cleanness and purity of the soul. And I thought: 'The fairness of this child cannot live with this body – and the filth of this body cannot live upon the child.'

CHAPTER 64

It is wholly blessed when man is taken from pain – much more than if pain is taken from man. For if pain is taken from me it may come back again. And so it is a wonderful comfort to the beloved soul, that we shall be taken from pain.

For it is his will that we shall be comforted beyond compare, and he showed this in these words: 'And you shall come up above, and you shall have me for your reward, and you shall be filled to the brim with joy and happiness.'

It is God's will that we should set the point of our thought in this blessed sight as often as we can, and remain there as long as we can, by God's grace. For this is blessed contemplation for the soul that is led by God, and greatly to his glory for the time it lasts.

And then afterwards, when we fall back into our sadness and our spiritual blindness, and in our frailty are prey to pains – both bodily and spiritual – it is God's will that we know he has not forgotten us.

And this is what he means by these words, and he tells us to comfort us: 'And you shall have no more pain, no more sickness, no more unhappiness, no lack of what you long for – but overwhelming joy and bliss without end. Why should it grieve you to suffer a while, seeing it is my will and to my worship?'

It is God's will that we take his commands and comforting as wholeheartedly as we can, and that we should take our waiting and our unhappiness as lightly as we can. For the lighter we take them and the less price we put on them, for love, the less pain we shall have when we feel them, and the more thanks and reward we shall have because of them.

CHAPTER 64

And so I understood that every man or woman who chooses God of his own will in this life, for love, may be sure that he himself is loved without end. And this love gives him grace.

For God wills that we should trust in this: that we shall be as certain, in hope, of the joy of heaven while we are here, as we shall be in certainty when we are there. And the more delight and joy we take in this certainty – with reverence and humbleness – the better it pleases him.

The reverence I mean is a holy, courteous fear of our Lord which is linked with humbleness. It comes when God's creature sees the Lord as very great, and himself as very small. For these virtues of reverence and humbleness are always possessed by those who love God. And they may be seen and felt, in part, whenever we feel the gracious presence of our Lord come upon us.

This presence in everything is most to be longed for, for it brings a wonderful certainty, in true faith and sure hope. It brings it by the strength of love, with fear that is sweet and pleasing.

It is God's will that I see myself as much bound to him in love as if all that he has done, he has done for me alone.

And this is how every soul should think inwardly of its lover: that is to say, the love of God makes such a bond between us that, when this is seen truly, no man can separate himself one from another. And this is why our soul ought to think that God has done all that he has done for him alone.

CHAPTER 65

And he showed this to make us fear him, and him alone. For it is his will that we know that all the power of our enemy is taken into our Friend's hand. And so a soul that knows this for certain shall fear none but him whom he loves.

He plants all our fears among passions and bodily illness and imaginings, and so although we are in such pain, sorrow, and unhappiness that it seems to us that we can think of nothing but our troubles and how we feel – as soon as we can, we pass lightly over them and count them as nothing.

And why? Because it is God's will that we know that – if we know him and love him and reverently fear him – we shall have peace and be in great rest, and all that he does shall be a great delight to us.

And our Lord showed this in these words: 'Why should it grieve you to suffer a while, seeing it is my will and to my worship?'

Now I have told you of fifteen revelations as God vouchsafed to bring them into my mind and renew them by the light and the touch (I trust) of the same Spirit that showed them all.

Of these fifteen Showings – the first began early in the morning, about the hour of four, and lasted in sure and proper succession, one after the other, until it was past noon.

CHAPTER 65

And after this, the good Lord showed the sixteenth revelation on the following night. This sixteenth was the conclusion and confirmation of all the other fifteen. But first I needs must tell you about my weakness, wretchedness and blindness.

I said at the beginning 'and suddenly all my pain was taken from me' and that I had no harm or discomfort from this pain for as long as the fifteen Showings lasted. And at the end it was finished and I saw no more.

And then I felt that I should live and linger on – and then my illness came back upon me. My head was filled with noise and din, and suddenly all my body was filled full of illness again, and I was as dry and as barren as if I had had no Showings. I moaned and writhed as I felt my bodily pain, for lack of comfort, either bodily or spiritual.

Then a priest came to me and asked how I was. I said I had raved that day, and he laughed loud and heartily. And I said: 'I thought the cross before me bled.'

And when I said this, the man I spoke to became grave and amazed. And then I was very ashamed, and astonished at my recklessness – and I thought: 'This man takes the least word that I say seriously, even though I saw no more than this.'

And when I saw he took it seriously and with such great awe, I wept, and was very ashamed, and wanted to make my confession. But at that time I could not talk about it to a priest, for I thought: 'How should a priest believe me, when I do not believe our Lord God?'

CHAPTER 66

I had truly believed at the time that I saw our Lord, and it was my will and intent to do so for ever without end. But, like a fool, I lost sight of it.

And I lay still until nightfall, and then I fell asleep.

And in my sleep, I thought the devil clutched my throat – putting a face near mine like the face of a young man. It was long and very thin. I never saw one like it. The colour was red, like new-fired tiles, with black spots in it like freckles, darker than the tile. His hair was red as rust, cropped in front with long locks hanging at the side. He grinned at me with a sharp look, showing white teeth – which made it all the uglier. He had neither properly-shaped body nor hands, but held me by the throat with his paws, and would have strangled me – but he could not.

This ugly Showing came in my sleep, unlike all the rest. And in all this time I trusted to be saved and kept safely by the mercy of God. And our courteous Lord gave me grace to awake – and I was scarcely alive. Those who were with me saw this, and bathed my forehead.

And then a light smoke came through the door, with great heat and a foul stink. I said 'Benedicite Domine! Everything is on fire!' And I believed it was a real fire that would burn us all to death. I asked those who were with me if they smelt any smell, and they said no, they smelt nothing.

And then I took to myself all that our Lord had shown me that day, together with the faith of holy church – for I saw it was all one – and fled to it for comfort. And soon everything vanished away, and I was brought to great rest and peace, without sickness of body or fear of conscience.

CHAPTER 66

Then our good Lord opened my inward eyes and showed me my soul in the depths of my heart. I saw it was as big as an endless world, and like a blessed kingdom. And by the conditions within it, I understood that it is a holy sight.

In the middle of it sits our Lord Jesus, God and man – a handsome man and tall: highest bishop, greatest king, worthiest lord. And I saw that he was arrayed in state, and gloriously.

He sits in the soul in rest and peace. And the godhead rules and governs heaven and earth and all there is – sovereign power, sovereign wisdom and sovereign goodness.

And Jesus shall never leave the place that he takes in our soul for ever, as I see it. For we are his homeliest home, and his dwelling-place for ever.

He showed the delight that he has in man's soul.

For it was made
as well as the Father had power to make anything,
as well as the Son knew how to make anything,
and as well as the Holy Spirit willed that man's soul
    should be made.

And so the blessed Trinity rejoices without end in the making of man's soul. For he saw from the beginning what should delight him without end.

CHAPTER 67

Everything he has made shows his lordship. And I understood at the same time how this is so, by the example of a man who saw the great riches and kingdoms that belong to a lord. And when he had seen all the lower treasures he was led to look above, to the high place where the lord lives. For it needs must be that his home is the most wonderful place in all his kingdom.

And so I understood truly that our soul may never have rest in things that are beneath it. And when it rises above all that is made, into itself, it may not stay looking at itself, but all its looking is turned upon God, its Maker, who dwells within it.

For his true home is in man's soul – and the highest light and brightest radiance in that city is the glorious love of our Lord, as I see it.

And what shall make us rejoice more in God than to see, in him, that he rejoices in the highest of all his works? For I saw in that same Showing, that if the blessed Trinity could have made man's soul any better, any lovelier, any nobler than it was made, he would not have been wholly pleased with man's soul.

And he wills that our hearts are raised high above the depths of earth and all empty sorrows, and rejoice in him.

CHAPTER 67

Seeing this while we are here on earth is a great pleasure to God and great help to us. The soul that sees this is made like him, and is joined to him in rest and peace.

And it was a special joy and happiness to me that I saw him sitting, for the fixity of sitting shows that he lives there for ever.

He gave me certain knowledge that it was he who showed all this to me before. And when I had looked on this carefully, then our good Lord told me these words most gently, without voice and without opening his lips:

'Now know this well – this was no raving upon you today.
But take all this and believe it.
Keep yourself in it, comfort yourself with it
and trust yourself to it
and you shall not be overcome.'

And these words 'you shall not be overcome' were said clearly and strongly to make us certain, and to give us comfort against all troubles that may come. He did not say:

'You shall not be tempest-tossed
you shall not be work-weary
you shall not be discomforted.'

But he said: 'You shall not be overcome.'

God wants us to heed these words so that we shall always be strong in trust – both in sorrow and in joy. For he loves us and delights in us. And so he wills that we love him and delight in him, and firmly trust him – and all shall be well.

And soon after this, all was shut away and I saw no more.

CHAPTER 68

And after this, the devil came back again with his heat and stink, and cost me dear – for the stench was so vile and painful, frightening and suffocating. Also I heard a noise, as if there were two people talking at once – holding a conference of great importance. And it was all a quiet muttering, and I could not hear what they were saying.

And all this was to lead me to despair, I thought – for it seemed to me they were mocking the prayers that are said loudly with the voice, but not with the devout intent and hard work that ought to be given to God in our prayers.

And our Lord gave me grace to trust him strongly, and to comfort my soul with spoken words – as I would have comforted someone else in trouble. And I thought that the effort it cost me was so great that it could not be compared with any physical strain.

I set my eyes on the same cross that had comforted me before. I set my tongue to speak of Christ's Passion, and to say over the faith of holy church. I set my heart on God with all my trust and all my strength.

And I thought: 'You must make an enormous effort now, to stay in the faith, so that you are not taken by the enemy. If only you would make the same effort, from now on, to keep out of sin, it would be a good and sovereign occupation.' For I thought, truly, that if I were safe from sin, then I was surely safe from all the fiends of hell and enemies of my soul.

And so the devil kept me busy all that night and on into the morning until it was about first light. And then they were all gone, all passed, and nothing left behind but the smell – and that still lingered awhile. And I scorned him.

And so I was delivered from them by the virtue of Christ's Passion. For by this is the fiend overcome, as our Lord Jesus Christ said before.

CHAPTER 69

In all this blessed Showing, our good Lord made me understand that the sight of it would fade. And it is faith alone that keeps this blessed Showing fresh – by his own goodwill and his grace. For he left me with neither sign nor token by which I could prove it – but he left me his own blessed words, which I truly understood. And he bid me believe them with all my strength. And so I do. Blessed may he be!

I believe that he who showed it is our Saviour, and that what he showed is the Faith. And therefore I believe it with rejoicing, as I am bound to, by all he said – together with the words that followed next:

'Keep yourself in it
comfort yourself with it
and trust yourself to it.'

So am I bound to keep this in my faith.

For on the very same day that it was shown, when the sight of it had faded, I denied it like a fool, and openly said I had been raving.

Then our Lord Jesus, in his mercy, would not let it be lost. But he showed it all again in my soul, with more detail, by the light of his precious love. This was said not just for that time, but also for me to build my faith on, when he said these words afterwards:

'But take it, believe it, keep yourself in it, and comfort yourself with it, and trust yourself to it. And you shall not be overcome.'

CHAPTER 70

For our faith is undermined in many ways by our own blindness and our soul's enemy – within and without. And so our dear lover helps us with spiritual sight and true teaching in many things (both inward and outward) so that we may know him.

And so, by whatever means he teaches us, his will is that we perceive him wisely, receive him joyfully, and keep ourselves in him faithfully. For there is no goodness above the Faith in this life, as I see it – and below the Faith there is no help for the soul – except the Faith. And the Lord wills we keep ourselves in it.

For we have to keep ourselves in the Faith by his goodness and his working. And it is by his permission that we are tested in the Faith by our soul's enemy, and made strong.

For if our faith had no enemies it would deserve no reward, as I understand our Lord's meaning.

CHAPTER 70

Glad and merry and sweet is the look our Lord God turns upon our souls. For he keeps us ever in his sight, living in love-longing for us.

I understand three ways our Lord looks upon us.

The first was the look of the Passion, which he showed while he was here in this life, dying. Though this look is sad and sorrowful, yet it is glad and happy – for he is God.

The second look is of pity, and sympathy, and compassion. And he shows this to all who love him, by looking after all those who need his mercy.

The third is that most blessed look as it shall be for ever. And this was shown most often, and continued for longest.

And so in times of grief and pain, he shows us the sight of his cross and his Passion, helping us to bear our troubles by his blessed strength.

And in times when we sin, he shows us the look of compassion and pity, powerfully protecting us, and defending us against all our enemies. And these two are those he shows most often in this life.

A third look is mingled with them, and that is his blessed look – which is, in part, like it will be in heaven.

And this look is a touch of grace and a sweet light of the spiritual life. It helps us to repentance and devotion, and with meditation – and all kinds of true solace and sweet comfort. This blessed look of our Lord God brings these to us, by grace.

CHAPTER 71

But now I must tell you of the way in which I saw deadly sin in those who shall not die by sin, but shall live in the glory of God for ever.

I saw that two opposites could never be together in one place. The two that are farthest apart are the highest joy and the deepest pain.

The highest joy that there is, is to know God in the clear light of eternity: to see him truly, feel him closely – having him perfectly, in the fullness of joy. And this is why the blessed look of our Lord was shown in part.

By this Showing I saw that sin is the absolute opposite of good – so opposed to it that we can never see the blessed look of our Lord clearly while we are muddied with any trace of sin. And the worse and more wicked our sins are, the further away we are from this blessed sight.

And so it often seems to us that we are in danger of death, in a part of hell, because of the sorrow and pain that sin brings us. And for a time we are dead, in that we cannot see the true sight of our blessed life.

But in all this I saw that we are not dead in God's sight, and that he never leaves us. But he shall never have his full joy in us until we have our true joy in him, and can truly see his lovely, blessed look. For we are ordained to it by nature, and get to it by grace.

CHAPTER 72

And so I saw that sin has power to make the blessed ones of endless life die for a short time only. And the more clearly the soul sees this blessed look, by the grace of loving, the more it longs to see it fully.

And notwithstanding that our Lord God dwells in us, and is here with us, and that he beholds us and enfolds us in tender love – so that he will never leave us, and is nearer to us than tongue can tell or heart can think – yet we may never cease from moaning, and weeping, and longing, until we see him clearly, and his blessed look.

For in that precious, blessed sight no sorrow can stay, and no good can fail.

And in this I saw matter for mirth, and matter for misery:

Matter for mirth, because our Lord our Maker is so near to us, and is in us, and we are in him – by sure safekeeping, through his great goodness.

Matter for misery, because our inward eyes are so blind, and we are so borne down by the weight of our mortal flesh and the darkness of sin, that we cannot see our Lord clearly, and his lovely, blessed look. No, and we can scarcely believe and trust his great love, and the certainty of our safekeeping, because of this murky darkness. And this is why I say that we may never leave off moaning and weeping.

CHAPTER 72

This weeping does not just mean tears pouring out of our earthly eyes, but it has a more inward meaning. For the natural desire of our soul is so huge and measureless that, even if we were given all the noblest things that God ever made in heaven and earth, and yet did not see the blessed look of God himself, we should not be able to leave off moaning and weeping inwardly.

And if we were in all the agony that heart can think and tongue can tell – all this pain should not trouble us, if at the same time we could see his lovely, blessed look.

And so that blessed sight is the end of all manner of pain to a loving soul, and fills it full of all manner of joy and bliss. And he showed this in the high, wonderful words when he said:

'It is I that am highest. It is I that you love. It is I that am all.'

We ought to have three ways of understanding.

The first is that we know our Lord God.

The second is that we know ourselves.

The third is that we humbly know how we ourselves stand as regards our sin and weakness.

And it was to teach us this that all the Showings were shown, as I see it.

CHAPTER 72

All the blessed teachings of our Lord God were shown in three ways – that is to say, by bodily sight, by words formed in the mind, and by inward sight.

As for the bodily sight, I have told what I saw as truly as I can.

As for the words, I have put them down just as our Lord told them to me.

As for the inward sight, I have told it in part, but I can never tell it fully – and so I am led to say more about it, as God will give me grace.

God showed two kinds of sickness that we have:

One is impatience and sloth, so that we make heavy weather of our toil and trouble.

The other is despair and frightened fear, as I shall tell later.

He showed sin generally, in which all evil is comprehended – but he showed only these two in particular. These two are the sins that most trouble and buffet us, as our Lord showed me – and he would have us cured of them.

CHAPTER 73

I speak of those men and women who, for God's love, hate sin and turn themselves to do God's will.

These are the sins we are most likely to fall into because of our inward blindness and earthly sadness. And so it is God's will that we should recognise them, and turn our backs on them as we do on other sins.

Our Lord himself gives us great help in curing these sins by showing us his patience in his hard Passion, and also the joy and delight he had in his Passion, for love. So he shows us, by his example, that we should bear our pains gladly and wisely. For that is great pleasure to him, and endless profit to us.

And the reason we are troubled by these sins is that we do not understand love. For though the three persons of the Trinity are all equal in themselves, the soul understood most through love. Yes, and he wills that we should look for, and delight in, love in all things.

And yet in this we are most blinkered.

CHAPTER 73

Some of us believe that God is all-powerful and able to do everything.

And that he is all-wise and knows how to do everything.

But as for believing that he is all-love and will do everything, there we hold back. And this lack of faith is what hinders God's lovers most, as I see it.

For when we begin to hate sin, and to mend our ways by the guidance of holy church, yet a fear still lingers and holds us back. This is because we see ourselves and the sins we have done before – and some of us see the sins we sin each day. For we do not keep our promises, nor the cleanness the Lord puts in us, but fall into so much mischief that it is a shame to see. And looking on this makes us so sad and worried that we can scarcely find comfort.

And sometimes we take this fear to be humility – but it is a wicked blindness and weakness. And we cannot scotch it as we do a sin which we recognise, because it springs from the devil's work. And it is contrary to truth. For of all the properties of the blessed Trinity, it is God's will that the one we should have most faith and delight in, is love. For love makes strength and wisdom gentle to us.

For just as by this courtesy God forgives our sins when we repent – even so he wills that we should forgive our own sins of senseless worrying and frightened fear.

CHAPTER 73

For I understand there are four kinds of fear. One is the fear of sudden attack that comes to a man because he is weak. This fear does good, for it helps purge a man – as bodily sickness can, and such other pains that are not sin. For all these pains are helpful, if they are borne patiently.

The second is the fear of pain, which shakes a man and awakes him from the sleep of sin. For while we are asleep, we cannot perceive the gentle comfort of the Holy Spirit until we feel this fear of pain – of bodily death and of spiritual enemies. And this fear spurs us to seek comfort and mercy from God. And so this fear helps us as a gateway to God and makes us able to repent, by the blessed touch of the Holy Spirit.

The third is doubting fear. Doubting fear draws us towards despair, and it is God's will that it is transformed to love in our hearts by true knowing of love. That is to say, that the bitterness of doubt should be turned into the sweetness of natural love, by grace. For it can never please our Lord to have his servants doubt his goodness.

The fourth is reverent fear, and none of our fears wholly please God except reverent fear. It is most gentle – for the more we have of it, the less we feel it, because of the sweetness of love.

CHAPTER 74

Love and fear are brothers, and they are rooted in us by the goodness of our Maker, and shall never be taken away from us for ever.

We have to love by nature, and we have to love by grace. And we have to fear by nature, and we have to fear by grace.

It is the property of lordship and of fatherhood to be feared, as it is the property of goodness to be loved.

And so it is right and proper that we who are his servants and his children should fear him for his lordship and fatherhood, and love him for his goodness.

And though this reverent fear and love cannot be separated, yet they are not one and the same. But they are twofold in nature and action – and we cannot have one without the other.

And so I am sure that everyone who loves, also fears – though he feels it only a little.

CHAPTER 74

All fears except reverent fear that come upon us, even though they come in the guise of holiness, are not so true. And this is how we can tell them apart.

The fear that makes us quickly flee from all that is not good, and fall on our Lord's breast as a child falls into its mother's arms – knowing our weakness and our great need, and knowing his everlasting goodness and his blessed love, seeking only him for our salvation, clinging to him with sure trust – the fear that brings us to do all this is natural, gentle and true. And all that is contrary to this is either wrong, or is mixed up with wrong.

And this is the remedy: to know them both and refuse the one that is wrong.

For the natural good we get from fear in this life, by the gracious working of the Holy Spirit, we shall also have before God in heaven – gentle, courteous and very sweet.

And so through love we shall be at home and near our Lord. And through fear we shall be humble and courteous before God – and both equally.

We should pray to our Lord to fear God reverently, and to love him humbly, and to trust him strongly. For the more and the stronger we trust, the more we please and honour our Lord we trust in. And if we fail in this reverent fear and humble love – as God forbid we should – our trust shall then be misjudged, for a time.

And so we have very great need to ask our Lord for grace so that we may have this reverent fear and humble love, by his gift, in our hearts and deeds.

For no man may please God without them.

CHAPTER 74

I saw that God can do all we need. And these are the three things we need, as I shall tell: love, longing, and pity.

Pity, in love, looks after us in time of need. And longing, in the same love, draws us up into heaven.

For the thirst of Christ is to have the whole of mankind within himself. By this thirst he has drawn in all his holy ones who are now in bliss. And, as he gets his living members, he continually draws and drinks – and still he thirsts and longs.

In God I saw three kinds of longing – and all for the same purpose. And we have the same in us – of the same quality, and for the same purpose.

The first, is that he longs to teach us to know and to love him for ever – since this is useful and helpful to us.

The second is that he longs to have us on high in his bliss, as souls are when they are taken out of pain into heaven.

The third is to bring us to fulfilment in joy. And that joy shall be fulfilled on the last day, and shall last for ever.

CHAPTER 75

For I saw, as is known in our Faith, that pain and sorrow shall be ended for those who shall be saved. And not only shall we receive the same joy that souls have had before in heaven, but we shall also receive new joy besides, which shall flow freely out of God and into us, and fill us to the brim.

And these are the good gifts he has ordained to give us since before time was. These good gifts are treasured up and hidden within him. For until that day, created man is not strong enough or worthy enough to receive them.

In this, we shall truly see the reason for everything he has done – and we shall for ever see the reason for all he has allowed.

And the joy and the fulfilment shall be so deep, and so high, that all men shall have such great reverent fear before God, in wonder and amazement – beyond everything that has been seen and felt before – that the pillars of heaven shall tremble and quake.

But this trembling and fear shall have no pain in it, for the glorious strength of God must needs be looked on by his creatures in this way.

CHAPTER 75

Weshall tremble and quake in fear because of the immensity of our joy. We shall marvel at the greatness of God the Maker, and at the smallness of all that is made. For it is seeing this that makes men wondrous humble and lowly.

And so it is God's will, and it is also proper for us – both by nature and grace – to understand and know this, and to ask for this sight and this deed, and for this to happen. For it leads us in the right path, and keeps us in true life, and joins us to God.

And good as God is, and great as God is, and as much as it is part of his godhead to be loved – even so it is just as much part of his greatness to be feared.

For this reverent fear is the lovely courtesy that is given in heaven before God's face.

And, as much as the way he shall be known and loved then, outstrips the way he is known and loved now – even so the way he shall be feared then outstrips the way he is feared now.

And so it needs must be that all heaven and earth shall tremble and quake when the pillars of heaven tremble and quake.

CHAPTER 75

I say very little about this reverent fear, but I know well that our Lord showed me no other souls except for those who fear him. For I know full well that the soul who truly accepts the teaching of the Holy Spirit hates sin more than it hates all the pains of hell, because it is so vile and horrible. For the soul that sees the nature of our Lord Jesus hates no hell but sin, as I see it.

And therefore it is God's will that we should recognise sin, and pray busily, and work hard, and humbly seek teaching – so that we do not fall blindly into it.

And if we fall, it is his will that we get up again quickly, for the worst pain any soul can have is to turn away from God for a time because of sin.

The soul that would remain in peace must, when another's sins come to mind, flee as from the pains of hell, searching into God for remedy and help against it.

For looking on another man's sin makes, as it were, a thick mist before the eyes of the soul, so that for a time we cannot see the beauty of God – unless we look on those sins and repent with him, and have compassion on him, and pray to God for him. For unless we do this, another's sin attacks, and batters, and hinders our soul.

And I understood this through the Showing of compassion.

CHAPTER 76

In this blessed Showing of our Lord I understood two opposites. One is the wisest thing that any man may do in this life – and the other is the most foolish. The wisest is for a man to do according to the will and counsel of his best and highest friend.

That blessed friend is Jesus, and it is his will and his counsel that we hold to him, and stay by him, our home, for ever – in whatever state we are in. For whether we are clean or dirty, we are all the same in his love. Through good and ill, he wills we never turn from him.

But because of the contradictions in us, we often fall into sin. Then this comes into our minds, by our enemies' prompting, because of our own folly and blindness – for they say this: 'You know very well you are a fool, a sinner, and also unfaithful. For you do not keep the commandments. Often you promise our Lord that you will do better, and then straight away you fall in just the same way – particularly into sloth and wasting your time.'

For this is the beginning of sin, as I see it, especially for those who have given themselves to God to serve him by holding his blessed goodness in their hearts. And this makes us afraid to come before our courteous Lord.

This, then, is how our enemy contrives to set us back with his false fears, because of our wretchedness and the pain he has in store for us. For he means to make us so worried and so weary by this, that we lose from our minds the lovely, blessed sight of our everlasting friend.

CHAPTER 76

Our good Lord showed me the enmity of the devil, by which I understood that everything that fights against love and peace – it is the devil and his crew.

And because of our weakness and our folly we have to fall, but because of the mercy and grace of the Holy Spirit we shall rise to even greater joy. And if our enemy gains anything from us by our falling – for this is what pleases him – he loses much more by our rising through love and humbleness.

And this glorious rising is such great sorrow and pain to him, because of the hatred he has for our soul, that he burns in envy continually.

And all the sorrow he would put upon us shall fall upon him instead. And this is why our Lord scorned him – and this is what made me laugh out loud.

And so this is our remedy – that we acknowledge our wretchedness and fly to our Lord. For the more eager we are, the more helpful it is to draw near him.

And so we say this in our minds: 'I know well that I have a sharp pain. But our Lord is all-mighty and can punish me mightily. He is all-wisdom and can punish me wisely. And he is all-goodness and loves me tenderly.'

And we must keep this way of thinking. For this is a lovely humbleness in a sinful soul – brought about by mercy and grace from the Holy Spirit – when we willingly and gladly take the lash and punishment that our Lord himself will give us. And it will be very gentle and easy to bear if only we will count ourselves well paid by all his works.

CHAPTER 77

For a penance that a man must take upon himself was not shown me – that is to say, it was not shown specifically. But this was shown – specially, and highly, and with a wonderful look – that we shall bear and undertake the penance God himself gives us, humbly and patiently, keeping his blessed Passion in mind.

For when we keep his blessed Passion in our mind, with pity and love, then we suffer with him as his friends did who saw it. And this was shown in the thirteenth Showing, near the beginning, where it tells of pity.

For he says: 'Do not accuse yourself too much, thinking that your trouble and sorrow is all your own fault, for it is not my will that you should be overburdened with sorrow and misery. For I tell you that, whatever you do, you shall have sorrow. And so it is my will that you understand your penance wisely – and then you will truly see that all this living penance works for your good.'

This place is prison, and this life is penance – and he wills that we rejoice in the remedy. The remedy is that our Lord is with us, looking after us, and leading us to the fullness of joy. For this is an everlasting joy to us in our Lord's meaning – that he who will be our bliss when we are there in heaven, looks after us here while we are on earth.

Our pathway and our heaven are true love and sure trust.

And he made me understand this in all the Showings, and particularly in the Showing of his Passion, where he made me choose him so strongly for my heaven.

CHAPTER 77

[175]

Flee to our Lord and we shall be comforted.

Touch him and we shall be made clean.

Cling to him and we shall be safe and sound from all danger.

For our courteous Lord wills that we should be as at home with him as heart may think or soul may desire.

But beware that we do not take this homeliness so much for granted that we fail in courtesy. For our Lord himself is the soul of homeliness, and he is as courteous as he is homely – for he is courtesy itself.

And he wills that those blessed souls who are within him in heaven for ever should be like him in all things. And to be exactly like our Lord is our true salvation and our perfect bliss.

And if we do not know how we shall do all this, we must ask our Lord – and he will teach us. For it is his own delight and his glory.

Blessed may he be!

CHAPTER 77

In his mercy, our Lord shows us our sin and our weakness by the kindly light of himself. For our sin is so vile and horrible that he, in his courtesy, will not show it to us except by the light of his grace and mercy.

He wills that we should be sure of four things:

The first is that he is our ground, and we have our life and being from him.

The second, that he keeps us safe by his strength and his mercy all the time we are in sin and amongst enemies who cruelly attack us – and we are in so much more danger because we let them in, and do not know our own need.

The third is how courteously he looks after us and lets us know when we have gone wrong.

The fourth is how steadfastly he stays and does not change his regard – for it is his will that we shall be turned towards him, and be joined to him as he is to us.

CHAPTER 78

And so, by the knowledge that comes from grace, we are able to see our sin profitably and without despair. For truly we need to see it.

And the sight of it shall make us ashamed of ourselves, and break down our pride and our presumption. For we needs must truly see that, by ourselves, we are nothing but sin and wretchedness. And so by the sight of the little we see, more is passed over which we do not see.

For he, in his courtesy, limits the amount we see – for it is so vile and horrible that we could not bear to see it as it is.

And so, by humbly knowing our sins through contrition and grace, we shall be broken from all things that are not like our Lord. Then shall our blessed Saviour wholly heal us and make us one with him.

Our Lord means this breaking and this healing for all of us. For he who is highest and closest to God may see himself – and needs to – as a sinner like me. And I, who am the least and lowest of those who shall be saved, can be comforted with him who is highest.

So our Lord has joined us in love when he showed me that I should sin.

CHAPTER 78

And because of the joy I had in looking upon him, I did not want to listen to that Showing – and our courteous Lord stopped, and would not teach me anything until he had given me grace and the will to pay heed.

And I was taught by this that, even though we are highly lifted up into contemplation by the special gift of our Lord, yet at the same time we needs must know and see our sin and our weakness.

For without this knowledge we cannot have true humbleness – and without this we cannot be saved.

And I also saw that we cannot come by this knowledge on our own, nor can we get it from our spiritual enemies – for if it were in their gift we should not see it till our dying day.

And so we are much in debt to God because he shows it to us himself, in a time of mercy and grace.

CHAPTER 78

And I also had further understanding of what he meant when he showed me that I should sin – which I took as meaning just me alone. But by the high, gracious comfort of our Lord that followed this, I saw that he meant all mankind – of which I am a member, as I hope, by the mercy of God – for the blessed comfort that I saw is big enough for us all.

And here I was taught that I ought to see my own sin, but not other men's sin – except if it might be a comfort and help for my fellow-Christians.

And in this same Showing, where I saw that I should sin, I was taught to be fearful because of my own lack of foreknowledge.

For I do not know how I shall fall, nor the size or measure of the sin – for I wanted to have known this, but I was given no answer.

But our courteous Lord at that time showed, surely and strongly, that his love lasts for ever and will never change. And he also showed, through his great goodness and his grace protecting us, that his love and the love of our soul shall never be sundered.

And so, through this fear, I have cause for humbleness that saves me from presumption. And in this blessed Showing of love I have cause for true comfort, and for joy that saves me from despair.

CHAPTER 79

All this homely Showing from our courteous Lord is a lovely lesson, and a sweet and gracious teaching which he gives us himself to comfort our soul. For he wants us to know, by his sweetness and homely loving, that everything we see and feel – both within and without – that goes against this, comes from our enemy and not from God.

As this: if we are led to become careless in the way we live, and in how we guard our hearts, because we know this love surrounds us, then we should greatly beware. For this leading, if it comes, is false – and we ought to hate it greatly. For it is nothing at all like God's will.

And when we have fallen, through our weakness and blindness, our courteous Lord touches us, moves us, and clasps us. And it is his will that then we should see our wretchedness, and humbly acknowledge it. But he does not want us to stay like this, nor does he want us to spend our time accusing ourselves, and he does not want us to despise ourselves.

But it is his will that we quickly turn to him. For he stands alone, and waits for us in grief and sorrow till we come. He is quick to clasp us to him, for we are his joy and his delight, and he is our salvation and our life.

When I say he stands alone, I am not speaking of the blessed company of heaven, but of his care and work here on earth – for this is what this Showing was about.

CHAPTER 79

In this life three things uphold us. By these God is worshipped, and we are helped, safeguarded and saved.

The first is the use of our natural reason. The second is the common teaching of holy church. The third is the Holy Spirit's work of grace in our hearts. And these three all come from one God.

God is the ground of our natural reason
and God is the teaching of holy church
and God is the Holy Spirit.

And they are all different gifts which he wants us to work at and attend to. For these work together in us continually, and they are great things.

And he wants us to understand these great things here on earth, as it were in a first reading book, or ABC. That is to say, we shall have a little knowledge here of the things we shall understand fully in heaven – and this is to profit us.

CHAPTER 80

We know in our faith that God alone took our nature, and none but he. And furthermore that Christ alone did all things that brought our salvation, and none but he. And, in the same way, he acts alone now in the last deed – that is to say, he lives here with us, and rules us and governs us in this life – and brings us to his joy.

And he will go on doing this for as long as there is any soul on earth that is destined for heaven – and he will do it so thoroughly that, even if there were only one soul left, he would be there alone with him until he had brought him to his joy.

And where I say he waits for us in grief and sorrow, this means all the true sorrow we have in our repentance and compassion – and all the grief and sorrow we have because we are not joined to our Lord. And all this is helpful, and it is Christ in us. And though some of us feel it seldom, the grief never leaves Christ until the time he has brought us out of all our sorrow. For love can never be without pity.

And whenever we have fallen into sin and forget about him and about keeping our soul safe, then Christ alone stands guard over us – and so he stands in sorrow and grief. So reverence and nature make it our duty to turn quickly to our Lord, and not to leave him on his own. He is here alone with us all – that is to say, it is only for us that he is here. And when I am a stranger to him through sin, despair or idleness, then I let my Lord stand alone, in as much as is in me. And it is the same for all of us who are sinners. But although it is true that we do this often, he in his goodness never lets us be on our own. But he is with us always, and tenderly pardons us, and always shields us from blame in his sight.

CHAPTER 80

Our good Lord showed himself in many ways, both in heaven and on earth, but I saw him take no place for his own except man's soul.

He showed himself on earth in the sweet incarnation and his blessed Passion, and he showed himself on earth in other ways – as when I said 'I saw God in a point'.

And he showed himself on earth in another way, as though on pilgrimage. He is here with us, and leads us up, and shall, until he has brought us all to his bliss in heaven.

He showed himself many times as reigning, but chiefly in man's soul. He has made it his resting place and his glorious city, and he shall never rise nor move from that glorious throne.

Wonderful and glorious is the place where the Lord lives. And so it is his will that we turn quickly at his gracious touch, rejoicing more in his entire love than sorrowing over our frequent falling.

For it is the greatest worship we can give him, that we should live gladly and merrily because of his love while we are here in penance. For he looks on us so tenderly that he sees all our living as penance. For the natural longing we have for him is an everlasting penance to us – and he mercifully helps us bear it.

For his love makes him long for us, and his wisdom and truth, with his rightfulness, make him allow us to be here. And he wills that we see it like this.

For this penance is natural to us, and is the highest – as I see it. For this penance never leaves us until the time we are fulfilled and have him as our reward.

CHAPTER 81

But here our courteous Lord showed the weeping and wailing of the soul, meaning this: 'I know well that you want to live merrily and gladly because of my love, bearing all the penance that may come to you. But, since you cannot live without sin, you have to suffer, for my love, all the sorrow, all the trouble, all the unhappiness that comes upon you. And this is so. But do not be too downcast by the sin that overcomes you against your will.'

And here I understood that our Lord looks upon his servant with pity, not with blame. For this passing life does not ask that we live completely without blame and sin. He loves us endlessly, and we sin continually, and he shows us our sin most tenderly. And then we sorrow and mourn with discretion and turn to look upon his mercy, clinging to his love and goodness, knowing that he is our medicine, understanding that we do nothing but sin.

And so we are able to please him, through the humbleness we get from seeing our sin, and we can faithfully understand his everlasting love, and can praise and thank him:

'I love you, and you love me, and our love shall never be sundered, and I suffer for your sake.'

And all this was shown me inwardly when he said these blessed words: 'I will hold you securely.' And by the great desire I saw in our blessed Lord that we should believe in this way – with longing and rejoicing – I understood that all that works against us does not come from him, but from our enemy. And it is his will that we should know this by the sweet gracious light of natural love.

CHAPTER 82

If there is a lover of God anywhere on earth who is always kept safe from falling, I know nothing of it – for it was not shown me. But this was shown – that in falling and rising again we are always held close in one love.

For in God's sight we do not fall; in our own sight we do not stand – and both of these are true, as I see it. But the way God sees it is the highest truth. And so we are much in God's debt because he shows us this high truth while we are here on earth.

And I understood that while we live here it is helpful for us to see both these at once. For the higher way of seeing comforts us inwardly and makes us truly rejoice in God. And the other, lower, way keeps us fearful and ashamed of ourselves.

But our good Lord wills that we see ourselves more in the light of the higher way of seeing, without forsaking the lower, until the time when we are brought up above, where we shall have our Lord Jesus for our reward, and be fulfilled in joy and bliss without end.

CHAPTER 82

There are three properties of God which I was able – in part – to touch, see, and feel. These properties give the whole of the revelations their strength and effect, and they were seen in every Showing – particularly in the Twelfth, where it is said time and again: 'It is I.'
The properties are these: life, love and light.

In life there is a wonderful homeliness
in love there is a gentle courtesy
and in light is our everlasting nature.

These three properties were held in one goodness – and my mind wants to be one with that goodness, and to cling to it with all my strength.
I saw this with reverent fear, and I wondered greatly at the sight, and in the feeling of that lovely harmony between our reason and God.
I understood that this is the highest gift we have ever been given, and it is rooted in our nature.

CHAPTER 83

Our faith is a light that shines by nature from our endless day, which is our Father, God.

By this light our Mother, Christ and our good Lord the Holy Spirit lead us in this fleeting life.

This light is measured carefully, to give us as much as we need in this night. This light is the cause of our life.

This night is the cause of our pain and all our grief, the grief by which we gain God's reward and thanks.

For we, by mercy and grace, steadfastly know and trust our light, walking in it wisely and mightily.

And when our sorrows end, suddenly our eyes shall be opened, and we shall see fully in a clear light. This light is God our Maker, and the Holy Spirit in Jesus Christ.

So I saw and understood that our faith is light in darkness, and this light is God our endless day.

CHAPTER 83

This light is love, and it is measured in the right amount to profit us, by God's wisdom. For the light is not so bright that we can see our blessed day, nor is it shut off from us. But it is enough light for us to live by profitably and work to deserve endless praise and glory from God.

And this was seen in the Sixth Showing, where he said: 'I thank you for your service and your suffering.'

And so love keeps us in faith and hope
and hope leads us in love
and, at the end, all shall be love.

I had three kinds of understanding of this light of love:

The first is uncreated love
the second is created love
the third is given love.

Uncreated love is God
created love is our soul in God
given love is virtue –

and it is the gift of grace which brings it about that
we love God for himself
and love ourselves in God
and love all that God loves, for God's sake.

CHAPTER 84

And I marvelled greatly to know this. For, notwithstanding our silly way of living and our blindness here on earth, yet our courteous Lord sees the work we do, and rejoices in it. And, of everything that we do, we please him best by wisely and truly believing this, and by rejoicing with him and in him.

For as truly as we shall live in the joy of God for ever, praising him and thanking him, just as truly we have been in God's thought, known and loved, since before time began, in his endless purpose that had no beginning.

In this love without beginning he made us, and in the same love he looks after us, and never allows us to be harmed and our joy made less.

And so, when the judgement is given and we are all brought up above, then shall we see clearly in God the secrets that are hidden from us now.

In that day not one of us will be moved to say:

'Lord, if it had been done thus, it would have been done well.'

But we shall all say with one voice:

'Lord, blessed may you be. For it is so, and it is well. And now we see truly that all things are done as it was ordained they should be done before anything was made.'

CHAPTER 85

This book was begun by God's gift and by his grace, but it is still not complete, as I see it.

Let us all pray to God for love, thanking him, trusting him, and rejoicing in God's work.

For this is how our good Lord wants us to pray to him – and this is what I understand from his own meaning, and by the words that he spoke so merrily:

'I am the ground of your praying.'

For I truly saw and understood in our Lord's meaning that he showed this because he wants it to be more widely known than it is, and through this knowledge he will give us grace to love him and to cling to him.

For we are his heavenly treasure, and he looks on us with so much love while we are here on earth that he wants to give us more light and comfort in heavenly joy by drawing our hearts to him from our sorrow and darkness.

CHAPTER 86

And from the time it was shown, I often asked to know what was our Lord's meaning. And fifteen years after, and more, I was answered in inward understanding, saying this:

'Would you know your Lord's meaning in this?
Learn it well.
Love was his meaning.
Who showed it you? Love.
What did he show you? Love.
Why did he show you? For love.
Hold fast to this and you shall learn and know more
    about love, but you shall never know nor learn about
    anything except love for ever.'

So was I taught that love was our Lord's meaning.
And I saw full surely that before ever God made us, he
    loved us. And this love was never quenched, nor ever
    shall be.
And in this love he has done all his works.
And in this love he has made all things profitable to us.
And in this love our life is everlasting.
In our making we had beginning, but the love in which he
    made us was in him from without beginning.
In which love we have our beginning.
And all this shall we see in God without end – which Jesus
    grant us.

Amen.

CHAPTER 86